BEYOND THE FOUR VARṆAS

BEYOND THE FOUR VARṆAS

The Untouchables in India

PRABHATI MUKHERJEE

INDIAN INSTITUTE OF ADVANCED STUDY
Shimla

MOTILAL BANARSIDASS
Delhi Varanasi Patna Bangalore Madras

First Published 1988

Published by the Secretary for
INDIAN INSTITUTE OF ADVANCED STUDY
Rashtrapati Nivas, Shimla 171005
in association with
MOTILAL BANARSIDASS
Bungalow Road, Jawahar Nagar, Delhi 110007
Branches
Chowk, Varanasi 221001
Ashok Rajpath, Patna 800004
24 Race Course Road, Bangalore 560001
120 Royapettah High Road, Mylapore, Madras 600004

ISBN 81-208-0459-7

Printed in India
by M.L. Gidwani at Gidson Printing Works, FS-5, Tagore Garden,
New Delhi 110027

FOR RAMAKRISHNA MUKHERJEE

CONTENTS

Preface ix

Acknowledgements xi

Abbreviations xiii

INTRODUCTION 1

Chapter 1: ENUMERATION, CONDEMNATION AND COOPERATION 17

Chapter 2: IDENTIFICATION, REJECTION AND SEGREGATION 37

Chapter 3: LIFE AND LIVING OF THE UNTOUCHABLES 64

Chapter 4: SUMMING UP 78

Notes 105

References 108

Index 115

PREFACE

THE deplorable conditions under which the greater part of the untouchables live as also the importance of the services rendered by them was brought home to me vividly through contact (either physically, that is to say, tangibly, or incorporeally, as through information in the media, etc.) with them in our day-to-day lives. Their appalling position and the thankless jobs they perform for society saddened me for a long time. This concern gave way to an interest which could only be satisfied by further research on my part.

Have we ever considered the fact that some of the respectable key-figures of Hindu mythology may be considered untouchables, according to the present categorization? To quote Ambedkar in this context: 'The Hindus wanted the Vedas, and they sent for Vedavyāsa who was not a caste Hindu. The Hindus wanted an epic, and they sent for Vālmīki who was an untouchable. The Hindus want a Constitution, and they sent for me' (Mathai: 1978: 25).

Winsome Bakha, the hero of Mulk Raj Anand's novel *Untouchable*, evokes the readers' sympathy, and his attempts to grapple with life bring out his utter helplessness. He is a naive and at the same time a pathetic figure, skilfully portrayed by Anand. And how Bakha was ill treated and humiliated by the upper caste Hindus! The question that always troubled me is: why or how the untouchables chose those jobs voluntarily which others avoided? The answer to that, I realized, lies in the past.

Over the years, untouchability has gained in proportion and importance. Now it is gradually assuming frightening proportions. But how, when and why did the phenomenon first appear in society? Was there some form of coercion (political and/or military?) or sheer necessity (economic?) behind its emergence? In this context, a parallel may be drawn with the undertakers in Europe. It is suggested that because of economic necessity they took up the job initially. However, even now they are looked down upon. One can also find our 'untouchables' with reference to those in China, Korea and Japan. Very little is known about them, except about those in Japan. The Buraku Liberation Research Institute has been working among the Burakus of Japan with a view to removing the discriminations faced by these people.

The problem of untouchability, as it appears today, is only the tip of the iceberg. How deep are its roots, and what shall one find when they are dug up? With this purpose in mind I ventured into this quandary where probably 'angels fear to tread'. With trepidation I discussed taking up an historical study of the untouchables in India with the late I.P. Desai and the late J.P. Naik. Professor R.N. Dandekar was one of the few who encouraged me in my venture, and also advised me to do the work single-handed, however long it might take. JP came to my succour and told me that the ICSSR would initiate the study, and hoped that subsequent funds would be forthcoming from other agencies since it would take a long time to complete the project.

During the last ten years, I spent sometime in the Max-Planck Institute of Starnberg and the Maison des Sciences de L'homme of Paris as a Visiting Scholar, apart from the annual six weeks' stay at the Fernand Braudel Center of New York at Binghamton as a Research Associate. I received office and library facilities from these research centres to work on this project. I am deeply grateful to those organizations for their timely and generous help.

The bulk of the material for this work was collected during 1976-79, when I was a Visiting Fellow at the Indian Institute of Advanced Study, Shimla. Professor S.C. Dube, Director of the Institute, and Leela Dube took great interest in my work, and we often discussed the problem together. Professor Margaret Chatterjee, the present Director of the Institute, kindly consented to my taking time off from present commitments to prepare the manuscript for the press. I duly appreciate her kind gesture.

It is, indeed, sad for me that after coming to the end of the tunnel IP is not there to offer his valuable comments. Nor is JP there to see the end-product of what he set in motion. I sincerely thank those who encouraged and helped me in my arduous task, and grieve over those who are no more with us.

Calcutta PRABHATI MUKHERJEE

# ACKNOWLEDGEMENTS

THE present study has been possible with grants from the Indian Council of Social Science Research, Indian Council of Historical Research, and Indian Institute of Advanced Study, Shimla. I am grateful to these Research organizations.

As fallouts from this study, the following papers have been published, details of which are in the bibliography:

(1) Toward Identification of Untouchable Groups in Ancient India as Enumerated in Sanskrit Lexicons;
(2) Panca: An Historical Enigma;
(3) A Passage to India;
(4) Status Determinants in Early Brahmanical Literature: A Note.

ABBREVIATIONS

Ācā. Sūt.	*Ācārāṅgasūtra*
Ait. Br.	See under *Ṛigveda Brāhmaṇa*
AK	*Amarakośa*
Āpas. Dh. Sūt.	*Āpastambiya-dharma-sūtra*
AS	*Arthaśāstra* (of Kauṭilya)
Aśv. Gṛ. Sūt.	*Āśvalāyana-gṛhya-sūtra*
Aṣṭ.	*Aṣṭādhyāyī* (of Pāṇini)
Atri.	*Atrisaṁhitā*
Av.	*Atharvaveda-saṁhitā*
Baud. Dh. Sūt.	*Baudhāyana-dharma-sūtra*
Baud. Gṛ. Sūt.	*Baudhāyana-gṛhya-sūtra*
BC.	*Buddhacarita* (of Aśvaghoṣa)
Bṛ. Ār. Up.	*Bṛhad-āraṇyaka-Upaniṣad*
Bṛ. Sūt.	*Bṛhaspati-sūtra*
Chh. Up.	*Chhāndyogya-Upaniṣad*
CHI	*Cambridge History of India*
Daśa.	*Daśa-kumāra-carita*
Gaut. Dh. Sūt.	*Gautama-dharma-sūtra*
HK	*Halāyudhakośa*
Jāt.	*Jātaka*
Kādam.	*Kādambarī* (of Bāṇabhatta)
Kaś. Vāmana	*Kaśika-vāmana-jayāditya*
Kāty. Śr. Sūt.	*Kātyāna-śrauta-sūtra*
Khadi. Gṛ. Sūt.	*Khadira-gṛhya-sūtra*
Laty. Śṛ. Sūt.	*Latyāyana-śrauta-sūtra*
Mait. Saṁ.	*Maitrāyani-saṁhita*
Mbh.	*Mahābhārata*
Mṛchh.	*Mṛchhakatikam* (of Śūdraka)
MS.	*Manusmṛti*
Nir.	*Niruktam* (of Yāska)
Rām.	*Rāmāyaṇa* (of Vālmīki)
RV.	*Ṛgveda*
SDS.	*Sarva-darśana-saṁgraha*
SK.	*Śāśvatakośa*
SKD.	*Śabda-kalpa-druma*

Sāṁk. Ār.	*Sāṁkhyāyana Āraṇyaka*
SPB.	*Śata-patha Brāhmaṇa*
SV.	*Sāmaveda*
Taitt. Br.	*Taittirīya Brāhmaṇa*
Vaikh. Sm. Sūt.	*Vaikhānasa-smārta-sūtra*
VMB.	*Vyākaraṇa-mahābhāṣya* (of Patañjali)
Yama.	*Yamasmṛti*
Yāska	See *Niruktam*
YV. Saṁ.	*Yajurveda-saṁhitā*
VS.	*Vajrasūci*
Vāsiṣ. Dh. Sūt.	*Vāsiṣṭha-dharma-sūtra*
Vāsiṣ. Sṁ.	*Vāsiṣṭha-smṛti*

Proud castemen of my unfortunate country!
Throw aside your pride of Caste—
Lest on your own unwilling head
Should be heaped the burning insults
That you now shower on others.
You have deprived the outcasts
Of the common rights of man,
With your very eyes
You have beheld their misery,
And yet you have refused to take them
to your heart—
But remember, please do remember!
—Some day you shall have to be
The equal of them all in ignominy.

RABINDRANATH TAGORE, *Gitanjali*
(Tr. Basanta Kumar Roy. *Harijan*, 5 August 1933)

INTRODUCTION

THE phenomenon of untouchability in India underwent a long and gradual process. Its emergence is an obscure area in the sense that not much work has been done on it to date. Compared to that, there are more studies on the contemporary situation of the untouchables, and measures adopted for their betterment are all based on these studies. But upliftment of the untouchables or measures to induct them into the mainstream of Indian life will not be effective unless the reasons for the emergence of untouchability in society are ascertained definitely. The urgency of the situation may be better realized if it is put in figures. The Scheduled Castes comprise at present more than twenty million people who constitute nearly ninety per cent of the 200 millions living below the subsistence level (*Statesman*, 7 December 1976, Calcutta, p. 12). Not all of the Scheduled Castes are untouchables. The untouchables are estimated to comprise one-sixth of India's total population of 68,38,10,000.

Obviously, this number was not so staggering before. But, in spite of their relatively small number at the beginning, the reason for their being untouchables did not go unnoticed It is, therefore, incorrect to assume that until very recently there has never been any criticism about untouchability or of the *varṇa* system for that matter. Looking back, one could almost assert that, from about the time when society was divided into four *varṇas*, questions had been raised not so much about the justification of ordering the society into such segments as to their subsequent immutability. Admittedly, the critical attitude toward this division in society often assumed the form of religious movements which questioned the Brāhmaṇical supremacy and preached equality of all men before God.

Thus, not only the ideological content of these movements should be analysed but their human component also, i.e. the *varṇas* involved in them, should be examined. Otherwise, the character and the real purpose of the movement may not be ascertained. But the two aspects of the problem in content and form, ideological and human, become difficult to ascertain, because almost all treatises reflect the viewpoints of their Brāhmaṇical authors who occupied a dominant position in society both intellectually and otherwise. Nevertheless, from fragmentary evidences, often inadequate and indirect, it is not altogether impossible to present an account of the origin and development of untouchability in India. From the description of different aspects of life of peoples and of society it is seen that there were social groups besides the four *varṇas*, and that their social position underwent changes over time. The alignment kept on shifting all the time. Ultimately, some from these groups were reduced to the category of the untouchables.

Untouchability occupies the extreme and the lowest position in the hierarchical division of Hindu society. From early times the peoples were not unaware of the injustice done to the untouchables. It is true that dissent seldom assumed the character of direct protest against the *varṇa* system, probably because that was too strong an institution to go against. Moreover, the *varṇa* division was sacrosanct and was strengthened by the Vedas, which imparted sanctity to the mythical origin of the four *varṇas*. Proceeding therefrom, other groups not only explained their emergence but also their respective location in social hierarchy in relation to these four *varṇas*. Cārvāka, an early materialist philosopher, had the temerity to question the very basis of this elaborate superstructure and openly defy the authority of the Vedas. Supposedly, Bṛhaspati stated: 'The three authors of the Vedas were buffoons, knaves and demons' (*SDS*. 1961: 10). Other religious sects like those of the Jainas, Ājīvakas and Buddhists, did not accept the Brāhmaṇical orthodoxy, and recognized the rights of the Śūdras and slaves, among whom there were presumably untouchables too. Tradition has it that the Buddha took a robe from a Pukkusa Mallaputta (Dutt 1971: 131), and that his last meal of pork or truffles was taken from a *cuṇḍa*, supposedly a blacksmith (or *caṇḍāla*?); the *caṇḍālas* and pigs were generally associated with each other. The Buddha died of food poisoning thereafter (Rhys Davids 1932: 260, n. 1).

However, none of these religious sects or reform movements, which appeared intermittently and continued up to the early part of the twentieth century and later came to be known as *bhakti* movements, openly condemned the caste system. The views of their leaders found expression mainly through a humanitarian standpoint. They treated the Brāhmaṇas and the untouchables alike in so far as their religious rights were concerned. The earlier movements, like the one led by the Buddha especially, seriously questioned the hereditary supremacy of the Brāhmaṇas. According to the Jain and Buddhist doctrines, specific virtues and not birth made one a Brāhmaṇa.

Significantly, some of the leaders of the *bhakti* movements like Rāi Dās, Kabīr, etc. themselves came from the untouchable castes. But even they did not openly violate the caste rules or oppose the system. Ultimately, the followers of these religious leaders ended up by forming new castes of their own (Briggs 1920: 206, 210 & c.) while remaining at the same time within the broad category of the untouchables. Therefore, the untouchables and similar social groups did not cease to exist in India. On the contrary, their ranks swelled numerically as time went on, when job specialization led to further fragmentation, each new group forming a new caste.

The problem of the untouchables, however, became a national concern when in recent times a political dimension was added to it. In order to examine untouchability, we have to look back in history. As mentioned earlier, the untouchables belonged to the lowest rung in the *varṇa* hierarchy, and they were always there. From time to time in history we come across one or other of these groups, in one context or another. One such group was that of the forest-dwellers (i.e. the *āṭavikas*) who received King Aśoka's attention. But other groups beyond the *varṇa* social structure did not require a political intervention, at least we do not have evidence of that. Instead, from about the later part of the eighteenth century we notice that the problem of some of these people had become acute enough to require prompt action on the part of the British Administration.[1]

One should, therefore, start with the emergence of the Scheduled Castes and Tribes, a broad category under which the untouchables are also included. We find the issue of the Scheduled Castes and Tribes becoming a live problem along with

(1) The gradual deterioration of the tribes and 'low' castes

resulting in intermittent rebellions and calling for measures adopted by the British Administration;

(2) The opinions and demands of the Scheduled Castes and Tribes as spelled out by their leader and spokesman Dr. B.R. Ambedkar; and

(3) The attitude and standpoint of the Indian National Congress as voiced by Mr. M.K. Gandhi.

A spurt of rebellions broke out, in which the armed uprisings of the Muṇḍās in 1789, 1797, 1812, 1819-20 and the Sāntāl Rebellion of 1855 (Ghurye 1963: 46, 40) were of more serious nature than others. Apparently, gradual encroachment on their land and their increasing dependence on moneylenders drove them to desperation and sparked off the conflicts. Since the tribes lost their lands mostly to the Hindus who were also moneylenders, the relation between the tribes and Hindus was neither friendly nor happy (*ibid.*, 25, 45).

In order to 'protect' the tribes and their interests, separate tracts of land were created for them under the Scheduled Districts Act of 1874. The Sāntāls were settled in one part of the Sāntāl Parganās; and under Section 52-A (2) of the Government of India Act of 1919, any other territory could be declared as a 'backward tract' (*ibid.*, 39, 91). The culmination of all the struggles, manoeuvres and bargaining gave birth to the Government of India (Scheduled Castes) Order of 1936, First Schedule to the Government of India Act of 1935.

Along with the measures taken by the British Government by categorizing the Scheduled Castes and Tribes, the problem of the untouchables drew the attention of the nationalist leaders like Ambedkar and Gandhi. Gandhi could sense the growing animosity between the caste Hindus and those listed under the Scheduled Castes and Tribes, but it did not assume a serious dimension until the policy of 'Protective Discrimination' in the form of separate electorate was proposed by the government. Thereafter, it formed an essential part of the national question, and Gandhi and Ambedkar took up their cause in right earnest. In the course of time, the question of untouchables and untouchability, and of similar other groups, took the form of 'caste struggle' as Ambedkar put it.

Both Gandhi and Ambedkar made attempts to understand and explain the phenomenon of untouchability in society. Its evil effects on Indian life did not escape their attention, and they viewed the phenomenon with growing concern. They completely agreed that the practice of untouchability should not be allowed to continue, and that the untouchables should have their rightful place in Indian society. While Gandhi held the firm view that the untouchables were Hindus, Ambedkar maintained an ambivalent attitude. This difference in attitude not only explains their respective approach toward untouchability and the methods suggested for its eradication but also Ambedkar's later acceptance of neo-Buddhism as a way out. To Gandhi the problem of the untouchables was one of the many evils the Hindu society was beset with; with Ambedkar it was virtually the only concern. Probably because of this difference in their approach, Ambedkar took his stand on historical facts and made exhaustive studies on the untouchables, while Gandhi was concerned with the contemporary situation and, primarily, with the removal of untouchability from Hindu society. Ambedkar, himself an untouchable, viewed the problem as an insider, so to speak. He took up the cause of his own caste(s), and was out to prove that there was nothing inherently evil or impure concerning the untouchables. Gandhi, on the other hand, was a caste Hindu (a Vaiśya), and by his own admission 'miscalled superior class or caste Hindu' (Sitaramayya 1946: I. 548). He assessed the problem from above and as an outsider, so to speak. To him the issue of untouchability was mainly a question of 'bettering' the lot of the downtrodden people placed in the lowest rung of social hierarchy. The respective caste ideology of Gandhi and Ambedkar may have influenced their outlook on the question of untouchability and its eventual removal from society.

Ambedkar made attempts to find out how untouchability emerged in India and also to examine some of the current theories in this context. His contention was that there was no agreed opinion on the definition of untouchability or precise reason(s) for its emergence; nor was there an expressed condemnation of untouchability till about the fourth century A.D. Ambedkar concluded that it was based purely on political and religious grounds.

As to who were the untouchables, Ambedkar started with the

specific term *antyavāsayin*, because this term happened to be connected quite often with the untouchables alone. The literal meaning of this term is one living at the end, outside or beyond (the boundary wall of a village/town/human settlement). His argument was that it was not true that the untouchables had once lived *within* the village before they became untouchable (Ambedkar 1969: 33-34; 42-43). Because nothing about their expulsion from the village had ever been mentioned anywhere, nor was it feasible to evict forcibly such a vast community and settle it outside the village boundary (see also Sharma 1980: 144).

What happened, in his opinion, was that the bulk of these people were from the conquered tribes who, when separated from their own tribes, were at a loose end and occupied a place outside the village boundary. Ambedkar called them 'Broken Men'. They comprised a band of so-called 'watch and ward' people who, in return of their services rendered to the village, received food and shelter from the villagers. In support of this hypothesis, he cited the case of untouchables in Maharashtra who even today demand their right to maintenance from the 'touchable' Hindu villagers, as it is one of fifty-two rights granted to them apparently by the Muslim kings (Ambedkar 1969: 43-44).

The rank of the outskirt-dwellers further swelled, Ambedkar continues, with the Buddhists joining them. When Brāhmaṇism regained its lost ground and Buddhism was on the decline, the Brāhmaṇas became powerful again. As a retaliatory measure, the Buddhists were treated with contempt and were allowed to live on sufference. But not all of them were reduced to this plight. Men from every walk of life embraced Buddhism, and those belonging to higher castes and/or having wealth remained unaffected. But others, probably those without any means of influence, were forced by the Brāhmaṇas to live outside the village. Still, none of them was untouchable yet (*ibid.*, 97-99).

Now, Ambedkar comes to the crucial point, i.e. the reason(s) for untouchability. In this context, he first discusses some of the current hypotheses about untouchables and points out their fallacies. Reasons offered for the rise of untouchability are mainly two: racial and occupational. Ambedkar discounted the racial theory with the help of physical anthropology, and proved that so far as physical characteristics were concerned there was hardly any difference between the Brāhmaṇas and untouchables belonging to the same region (*ibid.*, 76-80). Next, he examined the occupational aspect of untouchability because of the oft-repeated purity-pollution theory held by many, and concluded, by quoting from the *Nārada Smṛti*, that even when household slaves were engaged in sweeping the road, gateway, privy, etc. they were not treated as untouchables (*ibid.*, 83-84).

According to him, religion played an important part in this respect. From about the fourth century A.D. Brāhmaṇical orthodoxy took a firm stand on the society, and killing of cows became a punishable offence. Before that, at the time of Aśoka or in the lawbook of Manu, killing of cows was not a serious offence but a minor one (*upapātaka* in the *MS*). Gradually, however, excessive veneration for cows and cow-worship was advocated, possibly, as a reaction to Buddhism, and the Brāhmaṇas, therefore, promulgated the law against cow slaughter. It was no half-way measure. From killing of cows the Brāhmaṇas went a step further; they went against eating beef, although they ate it previously (*ibid.*, 114-22). Cows were now held sacred, and beef-eating was considered profane. Consequently, those who did eat beef came to be regarded with scorn in society (*ibid.*, 146-47). Ambedkar thinks that hatred for Buddhism coupled with contempt for beef-eating were the main reasons for making these people untouchables.

One may raise the question: 'why did not the untouchables accept the ban on cow slaughter or stop eating beef for that matter?' The point to note in this context is that, over time, the untouchable castes have tried to emulate caste Hindu manners and customs, thinking—erroneously though—that such imitation will raise their social status. In the opinion of Ambedkar, since the untouchables did not *kill* the cows themselves for eating their flesh but ate only dead cows' meat (possibly killed by others or those dying a natural death), the ban was not applicable to them (*ibid.*, 162-63).

Gandhi did not treat the topic of the origin of untouchability so elaborately as Ambedkar did, and, therefore, not so coherent an account is found in his writings. Yet, from the twenties onward, he often discussed the subject in public meetings, and wrote articles in papers from which one can form an idea of how he considered the problem. To him it was a terrifying reality '*imposed by custom*' (emphasis added), and he agreed that the untouchables led an animal-like existence (Gandhi 1339: 29, 58, 107, 19). It was, indeed, a shame that downtrodden people (i.e. the untouchables) had to live outside a village or a town (*ibid.*, 19).

Personally, he looked at the issue principally from moral and religious angles—predominantly a religious one (Sitaramayya 1946: I. 540). Untouchability, according to him, was the greatest stigma on Hinduism but was never a part of it. Nevertheless, Hinduism committed a sin by supporting it (*ibid.*, 29, 32). Therefore, with the reomval of untouchability Hinduism will be free from that blemish (*ibid.*, 65). In his own words: 'In attacking untouchability I have gone to the very root of the matter, and therefore, it is an issue of transcendental value' (Sitaramayya 1946: I. 552).

Since untouchability was linked up with the *varṇa* and the *jāti* divisions of Indian society, Gandhi frequently expressed his views on it. According to him, the *varṇa* division, as and when created by god, was justified but not in its present form (*ibid.*, 1, 89, 101), and the *jāti* division should be abolished (*ibid.*, 82).[2] Since the *varṇa* system was a divine institution, hereditary occupation should be followed by all (*ibid.*, 79). There should be no grading of 'high' or 'low' status in occupations or any ill-feeling among people following different occupations. Every occupation was important, however 'noble' or 'lowly' it may be, and its followers should be respected by all. Untouchability arose out of aberration of the *varṇa dharma*, for all men were born equal (*ibid.*, 104, 89, 75).

Gandhi expressed his sentiments by agreeing to call the untouchables 'Harijan', the people or children of the Hindu God Hari.[3] The main responsibility for removing untouchability, according to him, lay with the caste Hindus. It was their duty to serve and help the untouchables through personal contacts. This should be done with love and with a spirit of self dedication (to the cause of the untouchables), justice and righteousness (*ibid.*, 58-59; Sitaramayya 1946: I. 52, 226, 332). There should not be any discrimination against the untouchables. Temples, schools, colleges and jobs must be open to them (Gandhi 1339: 43, 75).

Addressing the untouchables, Gandhi asked them to observe cleanliness in order to counteract the argument that they lived in squalor and filth, to abstain from drinking alcohol and not to eat left-over food from others' plates (*ibid.*, 34-35). For the improvement of their lot, they should not seek redress from the government. If they did, that would spell a greater disaster for them. Change of their religion or resort to violence would also not solve their problem (*ibid.*, 47-48). Here one would point out that the 'untouchables' had been trying from very early times to free themselves from upper-caste domination by becoming Jainas, Buddhists, Muslims, Christians, and recently, neo-Buddhists, but with very little effect. Gandhi suggested that, instead of seeking redress through change of religion, they should be self-reliant and independent as self-purification alone would help them (*ibid.*, 44). They should be tolerant and patiently wait for the Hindus to change their own heart (*ibid.*, 43).

While discussing the topic of beef-eating, a fact very much held against the untouchables, he asserted that protection of cows was more important to the Hindus than the *varṇa dharma* (*ibid.*, 3). Hindus made those leave their society who ate cows' flesh, and it was then a justified step but not now. However, cows should be protected, because among all animals only cows had all along been and still are beneficial to mankind. By protecting them men protect the entire mute animal world (*ibid.*, 6).

In reply to a friend, Gandhi described his plan for a future society in broad outline (Gandhi 1927). There were four areas of activities in human society, namely, education, defence, production of wealth and jobs entailing physical labour (*ibid.*, 95). Let all men first turn into Śūdras, the lowest of the four *varṇas*, who supposedly performed the bulk of domestic and other types of manual and menial services. Gradually, the other three *varṇas* would emerge out of them. Very few would be really learned to become Brāhmaṇas, the spiritual and educational guardians, still less Kṣatriyas who would be the trustees of the people and give up their life serving the nation. The Śūdras would be the smallest in number, as no personal services would be required from them. The largest member, however, would be the Vaiśyas, because they would include traders, artisans, and peasants (*ibid.*, 91).

Apparently, the exchange of views regarding untouchability was not confined to written propaganda. The issue was taken up officially by the Indian National Congress, and, since Gandhi was an important figure, he influenced the organization to include the cause of the untouchables in its programme.

As early as in 1885, W.C. Bonnerjee had suggested in the first session of the Indian National Congress 'the eradication, by direct friendly personal intercourse, of all possible race, creed, or provincial prejudices' (Gupta 1985:151). However, it was in 1917 that the National Congress addressed itself to its members to remove untouchability 'imposed by custom upon the depressed classes' or suppressed classes so called at that time (Sitaramayya 1946: I. 52). In the course of time as the problem crystallized, so were the resolutions and programmes of the Congress. For instance, in 1921 and 1928, it was decided that every Hindu Congressman should try to remove untouchability and better the conditions of the untouchables by personal contact and by rendering services to them. Furthermore, Congressmen were urged to do all they could, and help the untouchables in every possible way (Sitaramayya 1946: I. 226, 332).

When the proposal of separate electorate for the depressed classes was suggested by the Government in 1932, Gandhi reacted vehemently against it in the following words (*ibid.*, 495):

> One word more as to the so-called 'untouchables'. I can understand the claims advanced on behalf of other communities, but the claims advanced on behalf of the 'untouchables' are to me the unkindest out of all. It means a perpetual bar sinister. We do not want the 'untouchables' to be classified as a separate class. Sikhs may remain *such in perpetuity*, so may Muslims and Christians. Will the untouchables remain untouchables in perpetuity? I would far rather the Hinduism died than that untouchability lived. Those who speak of the political rights of untouchables do not know India and do not know how Indian society is constructed. Therefore, I want to say with all the emphasis I can command that if I was the only person to resist this thing, I will resist it with my life.

Gandhi repeated his arguments against what he thought the dismemberment of 'untouchables' from the Hindu fold (*ibid.*, 509). In fact, even when backward areas were created by the British for the so-called aborigines, politicians saw in the attempt to keep India further divided within herself (Ghurye 1963: 129).

According to Gandhi, separate electorate was not the way to remove this 'bar sinister' (Sitaramayya 1946: I. 538).

Now, Congress mustered its forces against untouchability and in 1932 unanimously passed the following resolution (*ibid.*, 536):

> The Conference resolves that, henceforth, amongst Hindus no one shall be regarded as an untouchable by reason of his birth and that those who have been so regarded hitherto will have the same right as other Hindus in regard to the use of public wells, public schools, public roads and all other public institutions. This right shall have statutory recognition at the first opportunity and shall be one of the earliest Acts of the Swaraj Parliament, if it shall not have received such recognition before that time.
>
> It is further agreed that it shall be the duty of all Hindu leaders to secure, by every legitimate and peaceful means, an early removal of all social disabilities now imposed by custom upon the so-called untouchable classes, including the bar in respect of admission to temples.

On the eve of passing the bill on 'separate electorate' for the depressed classes, Gandhi decided to 'fast unto death'. He declared (*ibid.*, 551): 'What I want, what I am living for, and what I should delight in dying for, is the eradication of untouchability root and branch. . . . It is in order to achieve this, the dream of my life for past fifty years.'

Such an adamant attitude, both of Gandhi and the British Government, created a deadlock. Desperate attempts were made to solve this impasse by the leaders of the caste Hindus and the Scheduled Castes. A solution was found in the statutory reservation of seats, through primary election (Gupta 1985: 290-99).

However, all these attempts for the removal of untouchability were not much effective. One, therefore, cannot blame Ambedkar who, disillusioned mainly by the moral overtone of Gandhi and the National Congress toward untouchability, summed up the moves of the Congress initiated by Gandhi for the removal of untouchability as 'Congress's Plan to kill by Kindness'.

It is a sad commentary on the approaches of both Ambedkar and Gandhi that, even after several decades and in spite of time-bound constitutional safeguards, the problem, instead of abating, is gaining an impossible proportion today. Despite Gandhi's 'dream of life' to remove 'this bar sinister', untouchability is as live a problem now as it was then. The issue is a sensitive one, and it generates heat from both sides. In order to gauze the depth, intensity, magnitude and infectiveness of the problem, as ystematic study of every facet of the life of untouchable castes should be undertaken.

It is only from the beginning of the twentieth century that serious attempts are being made to study scientifically the position of the untouchables. While some readily came forward to study their contemporary position (to name only a few like Bailey, Bose, Briggs, Cohn, Freedman, Fuchs, Lynch, Mencher, Moffat, etc.),[4] some amount of hesitation and reluctance is noticed among Indologists and historians to study the past history of the untouchables. It seems as if the volume and magnitude of the task acts as a deterrent to a systematic study of the issues involved. Yet without a proper understanding of the genesis and development of this phenomenon, no measure or propaganda would be successful for the eradication of this pernicious evil.

With this view in mind, the present study attempts at tracing the origin and development of untouchability in Hindu society. This obviously limits our inquiry, so far as the time dimension is concerned, to *ca.* tenth century A.D., by which time the issues involved generated the problem faced in contemporary history.

As to who became the untouchables, there are several hypotheses. The most popular one is that some of them were of tribal origin, which is supported by Oppert, Fick, Bose, Sharma and also by Ambedkar who called them 'Broken Men'. This is probably due to the fact that at least one group of untouchables, the *caṇḍālas,* which exists in India even now, is identified with the *kandaloi*, whom Ptolemy referred as a tribe besides others such as *bhīlls, pulinda*, etc. (Bose 1942: I. 436; Fick 1920: 204-06; Oppert 1972: 155, 32, 80; Sharma 1980: 71, n. 3, 139).

Another hypothesis is that the untouchables originated from the family and village slaves (Ruben 1957: 98). This is based on the fact that within a family there were domestic slaves who did all the 'unclean' jobs, although they all lived within the same household. To begin with, in spite of the 'impure' nature of their work, the family slaves were not considered untouchables. But at the same time they were not allowed to cook food for the family (*ibid.*, 98-99).

The third hypothesis, which has been raised to the status of a theory, is ancient and indigenous, advanced by the Brāhmaṇa legists of India. According to them, the untouchables were born of miscegenation among four *varṇas*, the Sanskrit term for such children being *varṇa-saṁkara*, i.e. born out of mixture of four *varṇas*. Children born of hypergamous marriages (known as *pratiloma*) were worse than those born of hypogamous unions (known as *anuloma*), and the *pratiloma* children belonged to the category of the untouchables.

Three sets of hypotheses as regards the physical origin of the untouchables are thus available to us for our examination of the problem. While all of them need to be examined separately, for each may be valid to some extent, none of them alone can explain the origin of untouchability satisfactorily. Like the oft-quoted Indian parable of seven blind men and the elephant, these hypotheses deal with parts only and not with the whole. An elephant is to be seen to be believed. So may be the study of untouchability.

The reason, put forward as to why these particular groups of people become untouchable, is usually that of ritual purity and pollution (Haimendorf VIII in Fuch's book). The untouchables are ritually impure, because they follow unclean profession or vice versa. But did they voluntarily choose such loathsome occupations? Moreover, why those who are engaged in such occupations as basket-making, weaving, oil-pressing, etc. should be considered untouchables ? Therefore, this hypothesis needs a close scrutiny, because the purity-pollution factor may well be the effect and not the cause of untouchability.[5]

In continuity with the trend of argument in the same theory, it is proposed by some that untouchability is essentially of urban origin, as the kind of services rendered by the untouchables is required in towns and cities only (*ibid.*). This, however, does not necessarily explain their presence in villages today, or for that matter in the past. There are jobs requiring the services of scavengers and sweepers even in villages such as removing animal carcasses, cleaning streets, attending to cremation rites, etc. besides cleaning latrines which may be connected with urban settlements only.[6]

Since the present study deals with the phenomenon of untouchability in history, it is better to state at the outset how untouchability has been defined in it. Obviously, the primary attribute of the untouchables is that they are *aspṛśyas* to the caste Hindus, and the secondary relevant attributes are their segregation into distinct hamlets, non-commensality and non-connubiality with the caste Hindus. The term 'untouchability', however, is somewhat confusing as it may be temporary or permanent. For the present study, untouchability has been treated as a permanent phenomenon and as legally defined by the High Court. In the words of the First High Court which considered the question, it (i.e. untouchability) includes only practices directed at 'those regarded as "untouchables" in the course of historic development', that is, those relegated 'beyond the pale of the caste system on grounds of birth in a particular class' (Galanter 1963: 551 in Lynch 1974: 27).

The present study begins with the *Ṛgveda*, the earliest written Sanskrit document available. In order to denote those people who either composed the hymns themselves in the *Ṛgveda* or those who played the dominant role, I have used the word '*RV* people', or their self-styled name, the 'Aryas' (*vide*, Kosambi 1956: 75). I have deliberately avoided the word 'Aryan' because of its unhappy connotation in the recent past.

As untouchability makes sense only when it is juxtaposed against touchability of caste Hindus, the materials are collected mainly from the Brāhmaṇical (or Hindu?) sources, covering a period of about 2,500 years. Apart from those texts which are primarily sacred in character, greater reliance is placed on the evidence obtained from lexicons, *Nirukta*, grammars of Pāṇini and Patañjali, the *Arthaśāstra* of Kauṭīlya, accounts of Greek travellers and epigraphical materials.

I have left out the consideration of the Purāṇas but have consulted the epics to some extent. The former type of literature, although of immense historical importance, may prove too much to cope with at this stage of my study. Moreover, the main purpose of the study is to trace the origin of untouchability. This one can discern from the literature consulted, which clearly shows the main features and contours of this phenomenon as it emerged and took shape.

The task undertaken was not only a time-consuming one but often frustrating too. It was like sailing on an uncharted sea without a life-line. After a long and tedious wandering through the labyrinth of innumerable texts, one may find a word or a line about people not liked by that particular author. And even when the relevant material is found, one has to ask the question: 'Who writes for whom?' Furthermore, it is always uncertain whether the texts portrayed the 'ideal' or the 'real' situation existing in society. Nevertheless, one can probably draw a valid inference regarding the real situation by accepting the 'ideal' situation as maximizing the trend of a particular phenomenon the author had in mind. The limit thus indicated may refer to the positive or the negative aspect of the phenomenon.

What, however, is not easy while studying these texts for describing the emergence of untouchability is to arrange the available information under suitable chapters with well-demarcated phases. Often the types of literature cut across the accepted chronology of those texts. Because of the uncertain dating of those texts primarily, it is rather difficult to define clearly and demarcate these phases. The boundary lines are soft, and there will be frequent chronological overlappings from one phase to another.

What I have done, therefore, is to arrange the texts according to the landmarks in the account of the untouchables as recorded in these texts. Then the materials have been placed under relevant chapters. This might have ignored, in some places, the accepted chronology of certain texts. It was unavoidable. Instead of entering into the controversy at this stage as to their relative dates, I have thought it better to collect as much materials as are available, and to rely more on the recorded development of untouchables than otherwise.

Admittedly, in view of segmentation of society into numerous groups and subgroups, we should probe further than look into the Sanskrit literature alone. I have, therefore, made limited use of the Jaina and Buddhist sources. The Buddhist ideology was a serious challenge and posed a greater threat than the Jaina ideology to the Brāhmaṇical viewpoint. I have also had recourse to some archaeological findings validating the bibliographical materials, and to certain travellers' accounts. For instance, the (archaeological) remains of the Indus Valley, indicating the level of material culture and disparity among the people, can be of added help in describing the society of that time. It is true that history of that period is based more on conjectures than on facts. Nonetheless, valid conjectures made by piecing together the various strands of indirect evidence would result in a working hypothesis. Further researches may then prove or disprove the validity of arguments, and supply materials for the lacunae of the present study belonging to one of the shadowy periods of Indian history.

The next part of the study, if possible, will be based on oral history from the untouchables. That is to say, an empirical investigation is planned to find out what they themselves think about their origin, future, betterment of their lot, etc. Thus, we shall have views on untouchables from the 'top' and the 'bottom', and also from 'outside' and 'inside'.

Chapter 1

ENUMERATION, CONDEMNATION AND COOPERATION

FROM the evidence in the *RV* we find that besides the *RV* people there were other autochthonous groups in society. Their names appeared gradually in increasing numbers as and when the *RV* people came in contact with them. Simultaneously, we note that their relative position *vis-a-vis* the Aryas underwent changes over time.

It is not true that the *RV* people met with a homogenous mass or a single group of people. From the beginning names of several groups of people were cited in incantations, hymns and chants in the text. These groups forming the pre-*Ṛgvedic* society were mentioned sometimes by the regions they inhabited or by the occupations they followed, but more often without any specific statement about their habitat or the jobs they performed. In that case, we have only some names to go by (like that of the Dāsas) and a few details which the *Ṛgvedic* authors considered relevant to record. All such information, however, hardly help us in identifying them regionally or occupationally. Nevertheless, their relative importance to the contemporary society may be inferred from the nature and extent of interaction and varying degree of relationship existing between them and *RV* people.

We can broadly characterize the groups cited in the text as inimical, indifferent and friendly to the *RV* people. Some were overtly hostile, though important enough not to be ignored by the *RV* people. The intensity of hostility and animosity can partly be gauzed from the fact that some of the groups were so important that these were mentioned in the *RV* time and again. Some were probably neutral to the *RV* people, for they were mentioned without any adverse comments on them. There were others who were positively cooperative and helpful to the newcomers.

While one may argue as to whether these groups were the same, similar or different, there is no such ambiguity about one group at least. Unmistakably, the *RV* people, i.e. those whose opinions were voiced in the text, called themselves Arya[1], meaning thereby noble, of noble descent, or 'sons of god' (*RV*. I. 116. 6; 117.21; *Nir*. VI. 26.2, 9). Of all the unfriendly groups the Aryas came across, that of the Dāsa/Dasyu[2] appears to have engaged their foremost attention. If we go by the number of times different hostile groups were mentioned, then this group seems to be the most important as it has been referred about fifty times in the *Ṛgveda*.

The Dāsas were wealthy (*RV*. VIII. 40.6) and several towns were probably inhabited by them alone (*ibid*., IV. 32.10). They possessed vast tracts of land with no grazing ground (*ibid*., VI. 47.20), and the forest was a hideaway for thieves wherefrom the Dasyus lassoed the unwary travellers (*ibid*., X. 4.6). The Dāsas seemed to have control over water which was most likely the main source of drinking water greatly needed by the Aryas, or the Dāsas could have guarded the dams so important to agriculture (*ibid*., VIII. 96.18). The Dāsas were quite influential, and the territory where the Aryas stepped into possibly belonged to them; for Aryas were distressed to find themselves surrounded by the Dāsas (*ibid*., X. 22.8).

The Dasyus were considered like famine which was naturally dreaded very much (*RV*. I. 117.21; *Nir*. VI. 26.2). The Dāsas were ethnically and culturally different as their complexion was dark, and the Aryas considered them as subhumans, hypocrites, having no virtue, observing different customs and not performing any *vrata* (*RV*. II. 20.7; X. 22.8; 73.5). The military strength of the Dāsas is evident from such references as that Sambara was a Dāsa who maintained a vast army, and that the Aryas took pride in ransacking ninetynine (or 100 ?) cities belonging to the Dāsas (*RV*. VI. 31.4; 43.1; 47.2; VII. 99.5).

The Aryas were intent on killing and oblitering them from the face of the earth (*RV*. II. 20.7; VI. 29.6; 45.24; VIII. 70. 10-11; 76.11; X. 23.2). This was certainly an exaggeration. What was intended perhaps was that the Aryas must subjugate these people. But Dāsas were no mean adversaries. They were the most formidable enemies the Aryas encountered, and the real fight was between them and the Dāsas. There were two Dāsa kings by the name of Yadu and Turvasu (*RV*. X. 62.10). Other important personalities among them were Navavastu, Namuci, Bṛhadratha and Vaci or Vati? (*RV*. V. 30.7-8; VI. 47.21; X. 49.6). We may infer that the Dāsas were superior to the Aryas from the latters' assertion that they were equal to the Dāsas. The Aryas retaliated by depriving the Dāsas of the name of Arya (*RV*. X. 138.3; 49.3).

By the same token, i.e. by the number of citations, the next relevant group seems to be the Rākṣasas. They were mentioned nearly twenty times, and one entire chapter was devoted to them (*RV*. X. 87). Thus, they were either equally or more hated than the Dāsas. The Rākṣasas lived on or beyond the mountains, and could not or were not allowed to come near the *yajña* (sacrifice) performed by the Aryas (*RV*. IX. 15.6; X. 61.9). It appears that the Aryas were afraid of them and regarded them as no ordinary mortals who were even capable of overpowering the Lord Indra of the Aryas (*RV*. VII. 1. 19; X. 120.4). They had such strong feeling against the Rākṣasas that in one full chapter they gave vent to their desire to kill the Rākṣasas.

The Rākṣasas had been equated to disease (*RV*. IX. 85.1) as both were equally feared and avoided. They were physically repulsive, because they had big nails and often went naked (*RV*. X. 61.9; 87.12). They were, according to the Aryas, envious of other people, devoid of knowledge, inhuman, daring, eaters of flesh and anti-*stotra*, i.e. hymns (*RV*. VII. 194.1; IX. 71.1; X. 22.7; 120.4; 87.2). The Aryas wanted to destroy them completely and burn their womenfolk as well (*RV*. VI. 18.10; VIII. 35.18; IX. 86.48; 17.3; 49.5; X. 118.8), which is significant as in no other case were women thus singled out for retribution. Vṛtra was a Rākṣasa who seems to have resisted the Aryas for quite sometime, because the fight between him and Indra figured prominently not only in the *Ṛgveda* but continued in later literature too (*RV*. IX. 109.14; Keith 1934-35: 461-66; Macdonell 1963: 158-59; Ruben 113-26).

The third group that the Aryas had to reckon with was that of the Paṇis. They were referred to about thirteen times in the *Ṛgveda*. Their name cropped up mostly in connection with cows. They were alleged to have stolen and concealed the cows of the Aryas (*RV*. IX. 112.2; 1.32,11), and Indra was exhorted to recover them from the Paṇis (*RV*. VI. 39.2; X. 67.6). The Paṇis were reportedly wealthier than the Aryas, because cattle at that time indicated wealth. They were upbraided by the Aryas for being selfish, greedy, scheming, averse to giving gifts, ignorant, envious in speech and as non-performer of *yajña* (*RV*. VI. 51.14; 61.1; VII. 6.3; Macdonell 1963: 157). Only once were they identified with Dasyus (*RV*. VII. 6.3).

The Aryas never expressed such mortal hatred or animosity against the Paṇis as they did in cases of the Dāsas and Rākṣasas. In fact, it is not very explicit whether the Aryas were at all interested in subjugating these people. Their sole desire was to grab and/or recapture their cattle. There have been some attempts to identify the Paṇis by their occupation or the region they inhabited. The commentators explain these people as aboriginal traders who went in caravans and behaved like traders, i.e. they cheated others, and their nature was calculating, niggardly, etc. (Macdonell and Keith 1958. I. 471-72; *Nir*. II. 1.17.1, 5; 10-12). It appears that they, i.e. the Paṇis, were mostly cattle traders (*Nir*. II. 1.17.1), and Indra was requested to destroy those people who were by nature like Paṇi and Bekanatan (*RV*. VIII. 66.10). Thus, the enmity between the Aryas and the traders has had a long history which may account for the later degradation of this group in society. The episode of Saramā and Paṇi indicates that they lived beyond a big river which led some to conclude that the Paṇis occupied the region of Bengal. There is also another view that they were the indigenous people of the Indus Valley (Kosambi 1956: 67, 87-88). However, they supposedly resisted the onslaught of the invaders for quite a while.

The last group inimical to the Aryas was that of the Asuras. Approximately, their name occurred seven times in the *Ṛgveda*. The Suras were the gods, and their antonym was the Asuras. Two Asuras were cited by their names, those of Suṣṇa and Pipru, the latter a magician (*RV*. X. 99.9; 138.3). The Asuras also were wealthy people whom the Aryas wanted to conquer and kill (*RV*. VIII. 97.1; X. 53.4; 151.3; 157.4; 170.2). In spite of that, the feeling of rancour or animosity was not clearly expressed. It appears that the Aryas had little or nothing to fear from them (Macdonell 1963: 156).

Except the conjectural case of the Paṇis, the occupations or locale of other groups remain totally obscure. However, there was one group which was identified by the region it lived in, and both the group and its habitation had apparently not yet come under the influence of the Aryas, as is apparent from their repeated invectives against this group. Once it was argued that the cows' milk of those living in Kīkaṭa was useless since it was not meant for sacrifice, and Indra was invoked, therefore, to get the cattle belonging to, and seize the wealth of, Pramaganda (*RV*. II. 53.14).

However, Bekanatan, Kīkaṭa and Pramaganda are the three words whose meanings are still obscure. Bekanatan and Kīkaṭa are included in *Nighaṇṭu* IV. 3, under which all difficult and unexplainable or inexplicable words are enumerated. Bekanatan is supposed to be a foreign and unknown word which had been interpreted by Yāska (the author of *Nirukta* and the earliest extant authority on the *Ṛgveda*, who is placed before the Buddha) and others as those living on usury or in sin (Macdonell and Keith 1958. II. 73; *Nir*. VI. 26.10, 12). Wilson identified Kīkaṭa, which again is an unknown word, with South Bihar (present districts of Patna and Gaya), while Sharma identified it with Haryana (*Nir*. VI. 32.1. n. 5; Sharma 1980: 12). In later literature, the same region (i.e. Kīkaṭa, provided Wilson's identification is accepted) came to be known as Magadha (Macdonell and Keith 1958. I. 158). It is possible that Magadha was a corrupt form of Maganda or Pramaganda? Pramaganda was supposed to be a king of Kīkaṭa, who had an un-Aryan name (Macdonell and Keith 1958. II. 38). Others interpreted Pramaganda as a derivative from Maganda who lived on usury (*Nir*. VI. 32.1).

In any case, Bekanatan and Pramaganda appear to be either proper names or, as in the case of Pramaganda, the descendents of Maganda, and both were associated with usury. Kīkaṭa, on the other hand, was the name of a region, be it South Bihar or Haryana, whose people were un-Aryan, atheists and did not perform *yajña*. Unlike the other two, Kīkaṭa was mentioned as a land where cattle had been important.

These people apparently remained outside the influence of the Aryas or resisted their domination, and hence Indra was urged to grab their wealth. Yāska and two other commentators (commenting on the *Nirukta* and belonging to the first and fifth/sixth centuries A.D., respectively) justified this seizure on the basis that these people inhabited a land, which was occupied solely by non-

Aryas, and were, therefore, considered as atheists. The commentators used the prejorative term of *nīca-śākhā* in connection with these people. The word *nīca-śākhā* has been interpreted as those who were born of inferior families, i.e. *nīca vaṁśa*, and belonged to base lineage, i.e. *hīna-kula* (*Nir*. VI. 32.1, n 2, 2-7, 9). There is yet another explanation for *nīca-śākhā*, namely, that it denoted *soma* plant (because of its hanging branches) which had been associated with Kīkaṭa and Pramaganda (Macdonell and Keith 1958. II. 474). This plant was needed for preparing *soma* drink.

Besides these unidentifiable and doubtful occupational groups in the *Ṛgveda*, there are references to clearly occupational ones as explained by their names. For instance, there were *gopāla* (cowherd), plough-maker, *tvasṭā* (who built the upper part of a chariot), *karmāra* (maker of arrow), *vapta* (one who shaves beard), *takṣmaṇ* (wood-curver) *bhīṣak* (medicine man/doctor), and bard/reciter, etc. (*RV*. X. 19.4; 23.6; 93.12; 119.5; 142.4; IX. 112.1, 3, etc.). Indirectly, there are references to ironmongers who made axes and thunderbolt (*vajra*), and also to those who hunted birds and deer (Macdonell 1963: 55; *RV*. X. 53.9; VIII. 96.3; III. 45.1; VIII. 2.6). Since there are references to plough-makers and also to sowing of paddy (*RV*. X. 94.13), agricultural workers must have been present in society. Further, metals were needed for arrows, etc. and gold was often used as a simile (*RV*. VIII. 77.11), which indicate the presence of jewellers and metal workers.[3] But their specific names are missing in the text. However, whatever is not mentioned does not necessarily denote its absence in society.

Noticeably, no derogatory remark or hatred was expressed about these occupational units. For instance, a chariot-maker was not discriminated against, although cowhide was used for making a chariot (*Nir*. II. 1.5.13). On the contrary, they (i.e. the chariot-makers) were praised for their dexterity, skill and patience (*RV*. I. 130.6), and the same positive attitude is noticed toward agriculture (*Nir*. VII. 3. 19), breeding of cows and the occupation of cowherds (*RV*. X. 34.13; 19.4; 23.6).

Briefly, these were some of the more important groups the Aryas came across. But we do not know the exact position of all these different groups in the pre-*Ṛgvedic* social organization. Yet, the society of that period was apparently not at a very primitive stage, according to the archaeological findings. On the contrary, they point to a well-defined social structure.

The remains of the Indus Valley civilization indicate that the immigrants met with a socially stratified and materially prosperous people (Goswami 1936: 141-42; Kosambi 1956: 55; Piggott 1950: 168-70, 175, 263, 286, etc.), among whom inequality was present based probably on wealth and occupations. Their spiritual life, too, was not totally barren.[4] It is, therefore, not impossible that those who attained such a high degree of material culture were ordered into well-stratified social organization. Different types of dwelling houses also support this hypothesis.

Yet, in spite of their apparently high social order, they met with defeat at the hands of the *RV* people, which is generally attributed to the latter's superior knowledge of the art of warfare. But, in spite of their superior martial prowess, the Aryas possibly knew of no such divisions in society, since they were pastoral and nomadic people. Probably, the idea of a hierarchical structure was borrowed from the indigenous society to suit their own need.

In any case, one may argue that the Aryas found in northern India an already functioning society whose basis, except wealth and occupations of the people, is not known. Added to this, there were some occupational and regional groups, and also other unidentifiable people whom they met and fought with. Thus, to the Aryas the social arena was then polarized primarily between the conquerors and those to be or are already conquered. As the balance of power gradually turned in their favour, the Aryas no longer remained mere intruders but turned into settlers. It was then that they had to come to terms with the local people whose cooperation was needed for their survival. As new areas came under their control, it became increasingly necessary to establish a rapport with the 'natives' which was effected through coercion and/or appeasement.

Consequently, the Aryas were now in a position to induce the need for a restratification of society, so that a working relationship with different groups could be established for the functioning of the social order. In the process, it was only natural that the Aryas would include some of the 'friendly' autochthonous groups in their social organization, and exclude those who were 'hostile' to them. The factor of 'racial purity' also might have played a part in the exclusion of some people, as they desired to preserve their superior status from the 'dark-skinned' and 'snub-nosed' people.

It appears that the division of society under the *RV* people was mainly job-oriented, and the four *varṇas* emerged, each with specific duties allotted to them. As is well known, the division of society into four *varṇas*—Brāhmaṇa, Rājanya (also known as Kṣatriya), Vaiśya and Śūdra—first appears in the later part of the *Ṛgveda* (*RV*. X. 90.12), which is followed thereafter in all other texts. Clearly, this time the *varṇas* were hierarchically placed, as is evident from their origin, symbolic though it may be. The first three *varṇas*, i.e. the Brāhmaṇa, Rājanya/Kṣatriya, and Vaiśya were known as *dvija*. The Aryas arranged themselves into the first three *varṇas*, and, possibly, the local gentry which were friendly to the Aryas also was drafted to them (Kosambi 1956: 96-98; 1953: 200; Piggott 1950: 286-88). Most of the occupational groups were probably included under the Vaiśya *varṇa*. The Śūdra *varṇa*, in all probability, owes its origin to the non-wealthy, conquered and hostile groups. Probably, that led to the conjecture that the former Dāsa/Dasyu/Rākṣasa of the *Ṛgveda* formed the Śūdra *varṇa* (Ruben 1957: 95, n. 12).[5]

The *YV* is more elaborate. Besides the occupational groups of *karmāra*, *tvasṭā*, *takṣman* and *gopāla*, it mentions the following names: *ayogu*, *śailuṣa* (dancer), *māgadha*, *kitaba* (gambler, dice-player), *bidalakāra* (piercer?), *sūta*, *dhanuskāra* (arrow-maker), *iṣukāra*, *hīraṇyakāra* (goldsmith), *maṇikāra* (jeweller), *rathakāra* (chariot-maker), *Mṛgayu* (deer-hunter), *puñjistha* (fowler), *śvan*/*śvanita* (dog-owner), *kirāta*, *dhīvara*, *niṣāda*, *paulkasa* and *caṇḍāla*. (*YV*. *Saṁ*. 30.5-21; *Taitt*. *Br*. III. 4.1-17). Except the last three, all the names are evidently eponymous, and can be explained by their etymology.

The *SV* mentions the Dāsa, Dasyu, Rākṣasa, Asura and Paṇi. Nearly the same information is gathered about these people as form the *RV*. For instance, the Dāsa, Paṇis and Asuras were wealthy people, as ninety forts were held by the Dāsas, and treasures of the Paṇis and bounty of the Asuras are mentioned (*SV*. XVII. 3, p. 307; X. 3, p. 287; XII. 2, p. 253). But extreme measure was suggested only for three groups. They were the Dāsas and Dasyus who must be slaved, and the Rākṣasa who should be burnt down (*ibid.*, IX. 2, p. 179; XIV. 3, p, 223; V. 2, p. 260; IV. 5, p. 9; I. 10, p. 24; X. 3, p. 281, & *c*). The first two groups (i.e. the Dāsa and Dasyu), we are told, were without any rite (*ibid.*, II. 2, p. 162; XX. 3, p. 257). Only about the Dāsas a desire was expressed to take possession of them (*ibid.*, XIX. 1, p. 219).

The occupational group of *takṣman* (wood-curver) and the mention of a young physician are found in the *Atharvaveda* (*AV.* X. 6.3; 4.15). For the first time, a *kirāta* girl appears digging in the hills for medicinal herbs (*AV.* X. 4.14), which may indicate either her occupation and/or her habitat in the mountaneous region. While some of their names are self-explanatory, the affiliation of these people to *varṇa* hierarchy is not mentioned anywhere. In any case, the hereditarily determined occupation pattern was not rigidly followed as it appears in *RV.* IX. 112.3 that the son did not follow his father's occupation.

By piecing together all the information obtained from the Vedas we can have a comprehensive and also a significant picture of social/economic units in society. Specialization in occupation is noticed in apparently synonymous but operationally different terms. Specific groups are mentioned under the general terms of carpentry (*tvasṭā*, *bidalakāra* and *takṣman*), jewelry (*hiraṇya* and *maṇikāra*), weaponry (*dhanuskāra* and *iṣukāra*) and under hunting (*mṛgayu* and *punjistha*). Another noteworthy feature is that the people of the mainland seem to have established communication with the forest-dwellers as mention is made of people like deer-hunters, fowlers, etc. Again, two economic activities belonging to a settled economy are missing here, i.e. those of weavers and cultivators. Probably, the agricultural activity is covered by *viś* (later turned into Vaiśya?). However, there are references to agriculture and cultivators by such words as *kṛṣi* and *kināśa* (*Bṛhaddevatā* VII. 37; V. 9-10; VI. 138).

As noted earlier, the society had been stratified into four *varṇas* without clearly locating any of these functional arboreal groups in the social organization. It can also be inferred on the basis of available evidence that some of the non-Arya group of people were included either under the Vaiśya or the Śūdra *varṇa*, the latter being a large category, and an amorphous one for that matter. Therefore, it would be expected that the reconstituted four-tiered social structure would include *all* the people of the

Ṛgvedic and/or post-*Ṛgvedic* society, unless there were evidences to indicate that some social groups were left out. One such evidence emerges from the confusion created by the word *pañca* (i.e. five). Frequently, the word *pañca* and compounds like *pañcajana/pañcajāti/pañcaksti/pañcakṛṣti*, occured in the *Ṛgveda* or *Sāmaveda* (*RV*. III. 53.16; VI. 61.12; VII. 72.5; 75.4; 79.1; VIII. 32.22; 63.7; IX. 14.2; 65.23; 66.20. 101.9; X. 45.6; 53.4; 60.4; 119.6; 178.3, etc.; *SV*. II. 10, p. 52; XVI., 3., p. 148; XI. 2, p. 207). It is a very controversial and at the same time significant term, and we have difficulty in explaining it from the internal evidence.

In the *Nirukta*, a later text explaining some of the difficult hymns of the *Ṛgveda*, various current views are offered on this term. According to one school, *pañcajana* is explained as an aggregate of five, namely, Pitṛ, Gāndharva, Deva, Asura and Rākṣasa (*Nir*. III. 8.8; IV. 23.1; Lassen 1847: I. 796). Another view was more popular and was held by the philosopher and grammarian Aupamanyava[6] who was either a predecessor or a contemporary of Yāska (i.e. belonging to or before the seventh century B.C.) as he was cited frequently by Yāska (*Nir*. II. 1.2.17; I. 11.5). According to him, *pañca* stands for the four *varṇas* and group of people known as *niṣāda*, which was regarded as the fifth member of the four-*varṇa* structured society (*ibid*.). The third view held that it denoted the five families (of the Aryas) which entered the Punjab simultaneously, namely, those of Yadu, Turvasu, Druhyu, Anu and Pūru (*RV*. I. 108.8; Griswold 1971: 45; Kosambi 1956: 90).

Thus *pañca* raises several intriguing questions.[7] We note that all these interpretations do not conform to the then 'realities' described in the *Ṛgveda*. For instance, the first interpretation does not appear to be relevant for two reasons. First, prayer was offered repeatedly for the welfare and prosperity of the five and to let them have plenty of food and enjoy heavenly bliss. Moreover, they (i.e. the five) were also entitled to perform *yajña* (sacrifice). One can reasonably assume that this benevolent attitude did not extend to the Asuras and Rākṣasas whom the Aryas considered as their deadly enemies. Furthermore, since the Rākṣasas disturbed the *yajña* of the Aryas and were not allowed to come near it, it is hard to imagine the Rākṣasas, Asuras and the Aryas performing the same *yajña* jointly, unless, it means that the Rākṣasas and Asuras performed their own *yajña*. In that case, would the Aryas mention it at all? The second reason that weakens this interpretation is the inclusion of the Asuras and Rākṣasas with the Devas who are divine beings. Moreover, *pañcajana* indicates human beings alone and not celestial ones (*Nir*. III. 8.10).

Similarly, with the second interpretation, i.e. the *niṣādas* being the fifth *varṇa*, we face again two difficulties. The first is that nowhere in the *Ṛgveda* there is mention of *niṣāda*. The second difficulty is that *pañca* started occurring much earlier than the time when society was supposedly divided into four *varṇas*, for the *varṇa* division is found in the tenth book of the *Ṛgveda*, which is supposedly an accretion if not an interpolation. In other words, before the four *varṇas* emerged there was already in society a corporate body of five, i.e. *pañca*. Who or what were they?[8]

Coming to the third interpretation, we note that Yadu and Turvasu were interpreted as two Arya families. The *Ṛgvedic* evidence, on the other hand, shows them as two Dāsa kings, unless by strange coincidence there were also Arya families known by the same name.

On the other hand, all the three interpretations do make sense if later evidence is taken into account. In all probability, the three interpretations are offered and justified on the basis of the following references. If the first interpretation is related to a stage when the Asuras and Rākṣasas had been thoroughly subjugated and absorbed in the Arya social organization, then the prayer for the welfare of the *pañcamānava* (*AV*. III. 21.5) appears quite logical. The only exception is the Devas, which is yet to be explained.

The concept of five *varṇas*, as explained by the second interpretation, was probably propounded in society, when the Aryas found the *niṣādas* cooperative and helpful. From the *Yajurveda* (*YV*. 30.8) onward they figured quite often as a privileged and powerful group. In any case, the idea of five *varṇas* was quashed once and for all by Manu, a later legist, who stated that there could be only four and not five *varṇas* in society (*MS*. X. 4). Later commentators, like Skandasvāmī (commenting on *Nir*. III. 8.8), Medhātithi (commenting on *MS*. X. 4, 8), etc. tended to agree that the fifth *varṇa* includes the *niṣādas* who represented all those beyond the pale of four *varṇas*, i.e. the 'mixed-*varṇa*', *pratiloma* children and other groups.

Lastly, the third interpretation suggested Yadu and Turvasu, because they were mentioned in the text (*RV*. I. 108.8). But their names occurred in the first book of the *Ṛgveda*, which is supposedly of later origin than the rest of the text. That way this also strengthens the above inference that *pañcajana* denotes a later social development when influential indigenous elites (like these two Dāsa kings) were absorbed into their social organization. As to the common Dāsas, the prayer of the Aryas to have 100 of them (as workers or slaves?) points out to their eventual subjugation by this time.

In any case, the mention of a fifth category, be it the *niṣāda* and/or other autochthonous groups and individuals, indicates that during this period a working relationship was established between the *RV* people and those not openly hostile to them. Possibly, as time went on, the newcomers reached an agreement with neighbouring people without whose active help and support their survival would have been difficult. The motive behind launching this policy of cohesion was perhaps to extend their sphere of influence by collaboration or military conquests. Naturally enough, the initial contact of the *RV* people was with those living in areas directly lying across their path of conquests. Therefore, wherever their objectives were thwarted, both the region and its people incurred their wrath; and whichever group helped them in this purpose was suitably rewarded with their favour. Thus, whether a particular group was rejected or accepted by the Aryas was revealed through religious rites granted to it. For both enmity and friendship of the *RV* people against or with a group at this stage manifestly operated at the ritual level, that is, both by recognizing their participation in religious practices of the Aryas and also by granting them rights to perform certain rituals independently.

In this context, one may cite the example of some groups, particularly those of the *niṣādas*, *rathakāras* and *nāpitas*, for whom the Aryas displayed clear preferences to others. Possibly, some of these people were useful to them, and some voluntarily offered their cooperation. One may note here that the different roles assigned to them by the *RV* people were of special significance. With the *niṣādas*, the relationship appears to have been the closest. They were friendly to the Aryas who apparently gained much from having them initially as their allies. It may not be entirely wrong to assume that for performing their *yajña* undisturbed they required protection by the *niṣādas* (*Nir*. III. 8.1).

From the Sūtra literature and the epics we find the *niṣādas* as an independent and respectable group of people. They were a settled community, and there were villages and settlements occupied exclusively by them (*Ait. Br.* XXXVII. 7; *Laty. Śr. Sūt.* VIII. 2.8). The *niṣādas* were described as wealthy people in the epics. Rāma embraced Guha who was the chief of the *niṣādas* and lived in Śṛṅgaverapura (*Rām.* II. 50, 26, 33-34). In the anecdote of Ekalavya too, we are informed that he was the son of a *niṣāda* king and practised archery in a forest, probably because that was where they lived.

Puskara was the original home of the *niṣādas*, and they were worshippers of the Sun-god. A *niṣādasthapati* (either a king or the chief of the *niṣādas*) was regarded with respect in the Brāhmaṇical literature (*Rām.* II. 50.33; *Kāty. Śr. Sūt.* I. 1, 12). During *viśvajit* sacrifice, the sacrificer had to sojourn with the *niṣādas*, and *śrauta* sacrifice was prescribed for a *niṣādapati* (probably the same as *niṣādəsthapati* (Gopal 1954: 116). The person leading the horse for the *aśvamedha* sacrifice spent three nights among the *niṣādas*, where he was not to eat rice or barley or drink water from an earthern vessel (*Kāty. Śr, Sūt.* XXII. 1.30), which prohibition presumably did not cover other edibles.

Another favoured group was that of the *rathakāras*. They were clearly an occupational group. The highest laudatory remarks as regards occupations were reserved for the chariot-makers whose firmness and skill were favourably commented upon. They were supposedly skilful and patient too. They were also first mentioned in the *Yajurveda* along with *niṣādas*, and again in the *Atharvaveda* as subjects of kings (*AV.* III. 5.6). In the *Ṛgveda*, carpenters and wood-workers were mentioned as a group, apart from the *rathakāras*, which tends to make them a distinct group.

The *rathakāras* participated in the rituals prescribed by the Brāhmaṇas. The person travelling with the horse in a *aśvamedha* sacrifice was required to spend two nights among the *rathakāras* (*Kāty. Śr. Sūt.* II. 3.16; see also Ghoshal I. 134, n. 180). They were permitted to have *upanayana* (*Baudh. Gṛ. Śeṣa. Sūt.* II. 8.5) and also to offer *agnyādhāna* sacrifice. For the latter ritual, special *mantra* and particular seasons were specified (Dutt 1931: 171). All these privileges that they enjoyed indicated their importance in society. Their eminence was certainly not achieved in a day. It dated probably from earlier times and continued under the patronage of the Aryas.

For *nāpitas* there were quite a few synonymous words. In the *Ṛgveda*, a *vapta* is mentioned as belonging to an occupational group. In later texts, some more words like *kṣurin*, *muṇḍin* and *divākīrti* are mentioned. The last is explained as a person who performs his work during the day. This is probably a generic term used for the barber group as a whole. Other terms denoted the specialized jobs they performed. For instance, *kṣurin* for shaving and *muṇḍin* for tonsure.

On the ritual status of a *nāpita* opinions varied in the early literature. According to some authorities, the Vedas should not be studied where there was a barber (*Baud. Dh. Sūt.* XVI. 5.9; *Vasis. Sm.* XIII. 5). But others recognized the importance of a *nāpita* in *upanayana* (*Av.* VI. 68; *Khadi. Gṛ. Sūt.* II. 17.2) and also for shaving corpses. Another authority clearly stated that a *nāpita* should not be despised (*Aśv. Gṛ. Sūt.* IV. 17.16). During *soma* sacrifice, a razor was given to him by the priest, which indicated his proximity to the ceremony (*Kāty. Śr. Sūt.* VII. 2.12).

The varying degree of interaction between the Aryas, on the one hand, and the *niṣādas*, *rathakāras* and *nāpitas*, on the other, determined the order of priority in their relationship. As a recognition of the services rendered by them, they were allowed to participate in the religious activities of the Aryas. Consequently, there was also a correlation between the extent of cooperation and the ritual ranking assigned to them. With the *niṣādas* and *rathakāras* the relationship of the Aryas was also at the military and political level. One can understand why the Aryas valued the friendship of the *niṣādas*. They were not only politically powerful but they could also exert their influence on other 'tribes' and forest-dwellers in favour of the Aryas. Therefore, for political and military reasons it was useful for the Aryas to have *niṣādas* on their side. To warriors, chariot-makers' services were indispensable, and this became apparent in the relationship between the *RV* people and the *rathakāras*. Nevertheless, the chariot-makers and barbers were merely occupational groups and hence of limited number and influence. The *nāpitas* were probably of less importance, and, therefore, the relationship was only ritual. But all of them enjoyed privileges requiring a close cooperation with the *RV* people.

If we turn to technical literature like the *Nirukta* (Yāska) and *Aṣṭādhyāyī* (Pāṇini), and later scriptural literature like the Brāhmaṇas, Saṁhitās and Āraṇyakas, we find some of the aforementioned groups explained directly and sometimes also differently. All the evidences, however, noted social stratification as well as a hierarchical division of society. For instance, in the *Nirukta* the Brāhmaṇas are evidently the superior people to whom the goddess of learning approached (*Nir*. II. 1.4.1). Among them a *vipra* was one who was learned and performed rituals (*Nir*. II. 1.4.1; VII. 18.1; X. 39.1.5). At that time, it mas probably not imperative that a *vipra* must be a Brāhmaṇa, although later they became synonymous.

The word *viś* has been used for commoners, which was probably the predecessor of Vaiśya, who were like subjects of a king, surrounding and revering him, but not performing any sacrifice (*Nir*. VI. 22.9; VII. 26.1-2; XII. 24.2). The attitude of the Aryas to the Śūdras and their status may be inferred from the way Yāska interpreted their name. The word *vṛṣala* was explained as those (*i*) whose nature was uncontrollable like that of an ox, or (*ii*) who did not care for righteous acts—*dharma* (*Nir*. III. 16.22-23). Later this word has been used as an alternative term for Śūdras (*MS*. III. 154; VIII. 16).

The Rākṣasas were more deadly and more hostile than the Asuras. They killed people in lonely places, and moved about stealthily during nights. They were considered absolutely bad, and were aften compared with famine (*Nir*. IV. 18.9).

Then there was the broad division between the Suras and Asuras. They were supposed to be created from the better and the worse part of the body of the creator (probably mouth and thigh are indicated respectively). The etymology of Asuras is explained as those (*i*) who do not stay long at one place, which probably indicate their unsettled (nomadic?) life; (*ii*) who have been driven away from their habitat by the Suras (gods); or (*iii*) who possess *asu*, i.e. life-breath in their body. The Asuras, as their name indicates, are opposed to the Suras (*Nir*. III. 8.1-4; 20.9; X. 34.1-4), and the name seems to be a generic term for all those who were not friendly to the Suras. For the Asuras were bracketed with the Paṇis, then again with the Dasyus not only in the *RV*, but also in the *Nirukta* (XI. 25, 5) and the *Bṛhaddevata* (VIII. 24-38). And the enmity of the Aryas with the Dasyus is well known.

We can further assume the existence of other groups, although not specified as such. Thus, from the words like *ayas*, *loha*, *jyā* and *śmaśāna*, it is obvious that people were connected with these objects and places, but their location in the social stratification is not clearly indicated. The group that was held in contempt was Paṇi, sometime referred to as *vaṇij* (traders) which was a pejorative term (*Nir*. VI. 6.11; 26.11-12; II. 1.17.1, 5). Apparently, they were wealthier than the Aryas.

Among birds and animals, dogs (*śvan*) and crows were held in contempt (*Nir*. III. 18.4). This is significant in the light of later evidence of *śvapaca* as a social group occupying a very low position in society. The *vrātyas*, another group becoming a centre of controversy in later literature, is mentioned as hunters and/or beaters (*Nir*. V. 3.18).

In the grammar of Pāṇini some more names are mentioned. He refers to *barudha*, *kṣatra*, *kulāla*, *carman*, *takṣman*, *niṣāda* *sūta*, *caṇḍāla*, *ugra* and probably also to leather-workers, goldsmith and blacksmith, by way of illustrating grammatical formulae (*Aṣṭ*. IV. 1.97; 3.118; V. 1.15; 4.36, 95; VI. 3.70; 4.11; Vasu I, 781). Patañjali, while commenting on the *Aṣṭādhyāyi* of Pāṇini, further mentions *ābhīra*, *mṛtapa*, *domba*, etc. (*VM* II. 4.10; IV. 1.4). The occupations of *mṛtapa*, *domba*. *ābhīra* and *barudha* are not specified. The first two, most probably, were connected with corpses and crematorium, but the last two, the *ābhīra* and *barudha*, give no indication of their occupations.

In the body of the Brāhmaṇas, Saṁhitā, Āraṇyaka and Upaniṣad literature, forming parts of each of the four Vedas, we come across more names; and there we notice, probably for the first time, some indication of the occupations and habitat of some of them and also of the fear generated by at least one group, the *paulkasa*. New occupational names like *hastīps* (keeper of elephants), *aśvapa* (keeper of horses), *ajapāla* (goatherds) are self-explanatory; and so are *gṛhapa* (door-keeper), *surākāra* (wine-seller, vinter) and *vaṇijaḥ* (traders). The *dhīvara* and *kaivarta* were fishermen, the latter killed fish after collecting them on the bank of a pond. A *mārgāra* was a hunter and a *svanita* lived on showing tricks with dogs or led dogs. A Dāsa (of the *RV*?) has now become a fisherman and *carman* is obviously a leather-worker. The *kṣatra*, *ugra* and *sūta* were employed in the royal households. The first one was the main royal councillor, and the other two were eagerly waiting to serve a king after his arrival in a village (*Bṛ. Ār. Up.* IV. 3.37). Another significant term known as *ayogu* is noted, which is explained as a *varṇa-saṁkara* (i.e. mixed-*varṇa*) or a woman 'buying' or 'selecting independently' her husband (*Taitt. Br.* III. 4.1-17). A *kirāta* was qualified with a 'cave', a *caṇḍāla* with 'air' and *paulkasa* with 'terror' (*ibid*).

Regionally, we notice that Magadha still evoked contempt. For instance, Magadha was one of the regions which was not to be visited (i.e. *agamya*); and, if visited, one had to perform penance (*Baud. Dh. Sūt.* I. 2.14-15). It was condemned as a place where only 'outcastes', 'inferior Brāhmaṇas' (*Brahma-bandhu* and 'not-Aryans' lived, and here Brāhmaṇization made no head-way (Macdonell and Keith 1958. I. 116-17; *Sāṁk Ar.* VII. 13, n. 4; see also *RV.* III. 53.14; *Nir.* VI. 32.1-6). The Aryas hated Magadha so much so that one type of fever was wished to visit the land and its people (*AV.* V. 22. 14). Some more names of people were mentioned who still lived beyond the pale of 'civili-zation'. The sage Viśvāmitra banished his sons in anger to the outlying areas occupied by such people known as the *andhra*, *puṇḍra*, *pulinda*, *mutība* and *śabara* (*Ait. Br.* VII. 18; XXXIII. 6; Keith 1920: 307; Dutt 1915: 68).

Caṇḍālas were condemned as they were considered unfit even to receive the leavings from the plate of others (*Chh. Up.* V. 24. 444.4). Their low status is further indicated as they were equated to animals. We are told that for committing bad deeds in this life one would be born in the next life as a dog, a boar or a *caṇḍāla*. Probably, the descending order indicated not only the gravity of one's crime committed in this life (*ibid.*, V. 10.17) but also the status of a *caṇḍāla* which was inferior even to that of animals.

Thus, from the time of the *Ṛgveda* to that of the Upaniṣads, we note several phases in the interrelationship between the *RV* people and several other social groups. The *RV* people nursed an antipathy to Dāsas, Rākṣasas, Asuras and Paṇis. These people, except the Dāsas, were constantly being driven out of their homes and hearths, because they spoke a different language and did not follow the religion of the Aryas. In the subsequent literature, however, these three groups lost their respective identities, that is, they were not mentioned by their names. Only the Dāsas are found to continue with their name and function as fishermen.

The people of Kīkaṭa were hated, because they were anti-Agni and anti-sacrifice. But behind the denunciation were the facts like that the people of Kīkaṭa were ethnically different and wealthier than the Aryas in worldly goods. They possessed a large number of cows and were probably superior in warfare, because the Aryas waged a number of unsuccessful battles against them. So they must be subjugated and brought under control. Later, instead of Kīkaṭa, Magadha and its people were criticized, because they were not 'Aryans' and did not accept the suzerainty of the *RV* people for a long time. As pointed out earlier, the attitudes of the *RV* people found expression through religion, and peoples were appreciated or criticized in the light of their acceptance or rejection of the rituals or gods of the Aryas.

Gradually, in the course of assimilation and acculturation with the indigenous people, the *RV* Aryas ordered them into four major groups following specialized occupations, some of which were already present in society. While thus restructuring the society, some of the indigenous elites were suitably accommodated. For example, the Dāsas were deprived of the term 'Arya', suggesting thereby that some might have been treated otherwise. Moreover, the names of the two Dāsa kings were found in *pañca*, again suggesting an accommodating policy.

However, the largest group was that of the Śūdras, the last and the lowest of the four *varṇas*. This vast group included, among others those none too friendly toward the 'usurpers' of their soil, those already engaged in unskilled labour, and those inhabiting different regions and belonging to different ethnic groups. Subsequenty, more and more occupational groups were mentioned and specialization noted, particularly, in jewelry work, carpentry, animal husbandry, fishing and hunting. Possibly, most of them, especially those performing menial jobs, belonged to the Śudra *varṇa*, although nothing has been stated categorically. There were also 'tribes', forest-dwellers, those living in the fringe areas, and those forming occupational guilds and so on. In other words, the Aryas, through their alliance with the local elites, were powerful enough to bring these people under their orbit and place some of them in the lowest *varṇa*.

Apparently, the Aryas, and among them particularly the Brāhmaṇas, occupied the highest position and were at the apex, because not only the scriptures were composed and compiled mainly by them but many of the rituals described therein had to be performed under their guidance. Moreover, they were entrusted with teaching, which made them responsible for the interpretation and application of knowledge. That way the Brāhmaṇas not only enjoyed a place of eminence and importance in society but also retained their esoteric hold on their disciples. Other groups were ranked with reference to them, and the main criterion of status was, therefore, that of the nature and extent of relationship of a particular group to these people at the top.

In this apparently harmonious schema for alignment of all social groups, a discordant note was sounded by *pañca* which indicated the existence of a group (or a pool of groups) other than the four. Among all the interpretations already discussed, that of Aupamanyava deserves particular notice as he was the earliest authority. He described the *niṣādas* as the fifth member, and, according to general agreement, they were even lower than the Śūdras. Although the *niṣādas* had once enjoyed a high social status, later commentators mentioned them as a hunting and fishing community only. At this stage, there was no clear mention of particular groups belonging either to the Śūdra *varṇa* or to the *niṣāda* community. Moreover, in this large mass of undefined population, there was a still lower group known as the 'untouchables'. This group was placed in the lowest rung of the social hierarchy, and within it also there was further segmentation. But that came later.

In spite of hierarchy in society, as shown by the jobs allotted to the four *varṇas*, social mobility was not entirely ruled out. The functional aspect of the *varṇa* was more important than that of heredity. There was yet no evidence of total rejection of any group or groups by the four-*varṇa* society. Nonetheless, signs of further segmentation revealing the seeds of discrimination against certain groups in society were already present in the attitude of the *RV* people. Slender as it was, there was evidence of some activities being looked down upon. It was stated that all work did not suit every one (*RV*. IX. 112.1). For instance, working with plough and weaving came in for mild criticism. Initially, the *caṇḍāla* and *paulkasa* were mentioned and the attitude to them was neutral, although the latter was qualified with 'terror' (*Taitt. Br*. III. 4. 1-17). Ritual condemnation of *caṇḍāla* became clearer in the Upaniṣads.

Chapter 2

IDENTIFICATION, REJECTION AND SEGREGATION

IN THIS chapter we shall discuss, primarily, the evidence collected from non-scriptural (but Brāhmaṇical) literature to find out more about stratification and eventual rejection of some people by the dominant group in society. The clearest and probably the earliest evidence of a vertical division among the Śūdras is found in a technical literature, the grammar (*Aṣṭādhyāyī*) of Pāṇini. That way, a technical treatise is more reliable than statements/descriptions found in other normative texts. While explaining the rules for forming copulative compounds, Pāṇini, the grammarian, who lived around *ca.* 300 B.C. (Ruben 1954: 97; Macdonell 1962: 367) mentions some Śūdras 'who have not been expelled' (*Aṣṭ.* II. 4.10; Vasu 1.312). The obvious inference from this statement is that there were some Śūdras who were excluded or 'expelled'. Unfortunately, these Śūdras were not mentioned by their names.

Nevertheless, the issue of 'exclusion' was taken up by the commentators who, in the course of their debates, mentioned several groups to be treated accordingly. As a result, there was an elaborate controversy centering round the various aspects of the topic of expulsion. As to their living space, the commentators started with banishing them from the entire 'Aryavarta', i.e. the region stretching between the western and eastern India. Finding that not feasible, they were content to let some of these 'excluded' Śūdras (like the *mṛtapas* and *dombas*) to live outside the village, that is, near a crematorium. Ritually, they were not allowed to perform the sacrifices prescribed for others. But there again it was decided to let them have their own ritual practices. The social expulsion resulted in not allowing them to use the same vessel for eating. Either earthen vessels should be reserved for them, which could be thrown away after use or they could use metal vessels which became clean and 'pure' after being wiped with ashes. But still they were all Śūdras.

Kauṭilya (in his *Arthaśāstra*) furnishes, for the first time, additional information about several groups of people, some new and some already mentioned, their position in the *varṇa* society, dwelling places, occupations, etc. The following names are found in the *Arthaśāstra: āṭavika*, *kirāta*, *śabara*, *pulinda*, *araṇyacāra* (i.e. those who roam in the forest), *mlechha*, *caṇḍāla*, *svaganin* and *śvapaca*. There were some people known as *lubdhaka* who worked as beaters and protected cattle from wild beasts.

The king appears to have had little or no control over the forest territory and also on those who inhabited it. In this context, the *āṭavikas*, i.e. those who lived in *aṭavī* (forest) figured frequently. The king was advised by Kauṭilya not to trust the *āṭavika* (*AS*. IV. II; V. 1.6; VII. 10; IX. 2.3; XIII. 3). They took away cattle belonging to a king (*AS*. II. 29), and destroyed forts and country parts of a kingdom (*AS*. III. 12). A king was, therefore, advised not to attack a country which was under the influence of the *āṭavikas* (*AS*. II. 1). He should immediately be informed by his secret agents if any suspicious movements were noted among them near his territory (*AS*. II. 34). However, those *āṭavikas* who accepted the political authority of a king served him as soldiers (*AS*. II. 33; VII. 7.14; IX. 2). This mistrust of an *āṭavika* was not entirely unfounded as we find from later evidence. Aśoka, who was paternalistic in his attitude toward all his subjects, threatened the *āṭavikas* in no uncertain terms. From Major Rock Edict No. XIII of Aśoka it is noted that after the Kaliṅga war the forest people were threatened to be killed should they fail to obey him (Bhandarkar 1969: 210; Thapar 1963: 256).

Another group of people, which was obviously connected with dogs, is frequently mentioned in the *Arthaśāstra*. This group is expressed by such terms as *śvan*, *śvapati*, *svaganin*, *śvagaṇika*, etc. (*AS*. I. 14; II. 34; IV. 5). But their emergence in the *Arthaśāstra* is not a new phenomenon. One may note that in the *RV* Saramā was a canine goddess whose descendents were known as *sārameya*, i.e. dogs. She was sent to the Paṇis to restore the stolen cows of the Aryas. To the *RV* people dogs were essential for guarding their homes as well as for hunting (Piggott 1950: 265), and hence Sarama was revered as a minor deity.

Between the time of the *RV* and of the *AS*, however, *śvan* group of people, for some reason, lost their eminent social position but not their usefulness to society. Even in those days breeding and rearing of dogs were important, and from later evidence we find that dogs were of very high quality in India, and they were a match even for tigers. In the Greek accounts, there is a reference, probably, to the *śvapacas*. These people were mentioned as *śuna-mukha*, i.e. dog-faced/headed, and their estimated number was 1,20,000 (McCrindle 1973: 87, 52). The *śuna-mukhas* had dogs which were of great size and fought even with tigers (*ibid*., 9, 36, 37, 85). Alexander witnessed such a fight where a tiger was ultimately overpowered and killed by a dog. Because of their superior quality Alexander took away with him 150 dogs when he left India (Majumdar 1960: 259-60; Stutley 1977: 294). Therefore, one may assume that the number of people engaged in breeding dogs was not inconsiderable; at any rate, not unimportant in society.[1]

Thus, we have the names of various occupational groups existing in society besides those of the four *varṇas*. Broadly speaking, they may be grouped as traders, artisans and craftsmen, hunters, animal-keepers, performing artists and those concerned with forest products. Some of them were engaged by the king and others might have been self-employed. In addition to these specified groups, there were other unspecified ones like *kirāta*, *mlechha*, *niṣāda*, *mṛtapa*, *domba*, *caṇḍāla*, *andhra*, *puṇḍra*, *pulinda*, *ābhīra*, and *śabara*.

Some of the latter set of groups like *śabara*, *pulinda*, etc. were later identified as tribes besides those of *niṣāda* and *kirāta*, and some others were known vaguely as forest-dwellers or working in forests. The *kirātas* were described by the Greeks as pygmies (McCrindle 1973: 87-88) and in Sanskrit as *alpa-tanu*, i.e. of short stature, and not as dwarfs (Ganapati Sastri to *AS*. I. 12; XIV. I). They were supposedly swarthy, deformed, snub-nosed, and wore long hair and large beards (McCrindle 1973: 15, 87-90). We do not know definitely whether these groups were mutually exclusive and whether their occupations were hereditarily determined, or intermural mobility was allowed.

About the remaining ones nothing definite is known. Among them the *caṇḍālas* (and also the *śvapacas*) denote the most relevant group for our study. While looking for those who constituted the 'excluded' (*niravasitā*) population of Pāṇini, the *caṇḍālas* fall into a pattern because they were probably the earliest ones to be on the wrong side of the *varṇa* society. The *caṇḍālas* denoted the first group which was considered the lowest of all, as is evident from statements like that a Brāhmaṇa guilty of certain crimes was to be born a *caṇḍāla* (among other things) in the next birth. However, in spite of the open condemnation in the Upaniṣad, food was offered to the *caṇḍālas* (and also to the dogs) by a householder after *vaiśvadeva* (*Āpas. Dh. Sūt.* II. 4.9.5), and they, along with the *śvapacas*, were purified by the incantation of *praṇavamantra* (*Baud. Gṛ. Śeṣa. Sūt.* III. 1.3).

Gradually, the grouping as well as ranking of the *caṇḍāla/śvapaca* become apparent not only from the attitude to them but also from various discriminatory measures. As time went on, various injunctions revealed the contempt (of the Brāhamaṇas?) for these people. To begin with, there was a general condemnation of *caṇḍālas* as being the worst of all (*MS*. X. 16, 26; see also *SKD*. II. 902, where *Agnipurāṇa* was quoted in support of this view). The notion of ceremonial purity gained enormous importance during the Brāhmaṇa literature period (Dutt 1931: I. 132), which logically implied ceremonial impurity of certain other people; and, in this respect, the *caṇḍālās* and/or *śvapacas* were the first targets. Kauṭilya labelled them as *aśuci*, that is, impure (*AS*. III. 19).

Subsequently, there were specific injunctions against them at the ritual level and thereafter evidences of their degradation, and probably of their segregation, too. The Vedas should not be studied in a village which was inhabited by *caṇḍālas* or if their presence was noticed on the outskirt of a village (*Āpas. Dh. Śut.* 1.3.9.15). Food offered in *śrāddha* would be polluted if seen by a *caṇḍāla*; others in this context of visual prohibition being dogs, crows and *patitas* (*Gaut. Dh. Sūt.* II. 6.25). The *caṇḍālas* were *amedhyas*, i.e. unholy, and sacrificial vessels became impure by their touch. Kindled wood (*araṇi*) was defiled by the touch of a *caṇḍāla*, and also by that of a Śūdra, *patita*, a woman in her monthly course, a crow, a donkey, etc. (*Śrauta Kośa* I. II. 27.8). Sacred fire became impure if it came in contact with fire belonging to a *caṇḍāla* and an expiation was prescribed for it (*Kāty. Śr. Sūt.* XXV. 4.34; XII. 4.4).

And gradually, the 'untouchable' aspect of their life was

brought under focus. One touching a *caṇḍāla* (and others like a corpse, a *patita*, etc.) should bathe with one's clothes on (*Vāsiṣtha* XXIII. 33; *Visṇu* XXII. 69). To touch, talk with or even to look at a *caṇḍāla* made one undergo penance (*Āpas. Dh. Sūt.* II. 1.2. 8). For touching an Arya woman a *caṇḍāla* was fined one hundred *paṇas*, and for adultery with her a *śvapaca* was sentenced to death (*AS.* IV. 13). A *mātaṅga* girl (same as *caṇḍāla*) was appreciated for her physical beauty, although she was contaminated by her caste, *mātaṅga-jāti-sparśa-doṣa* (*Kādam.* 38).

The *caṇḍālas* were differentiated not only from the four *varṇas* but also from other groups as well, and their lowest position was underlined. They were to have separate wells, exclusively for their own use and not for any one else (*AS.* I. 14). A Brāhmaṇa committing adultery with a *caṇḍāla* woman became *caṇḍāla/patita*, or he performed an expiatory rite (*Baud. Dh. Sūt.* II. 2.4, 13-14). A Śūdra having an adulterous connection with a *śvapaca* woman was degraded to her caste (*AS.* IV. 13). For stealing animals belonging to a *caṇḍāla* (or to any other *araṇyacara*) one has to pay only half of the prescribed fines (*AS.* IV. 10).

The *caṇḍālas* and *śvapacas* must not stay long at one place. They should not enter a village at night, and during the day they were allowed entry into a village only if they carried some identification marks from the king (*MS.* X. 51-52, 55). Fa-Hien noted that the *caṇḍālas* announced their entry into a village by beating drums (Beal 1869: 55). For food they depended on others which should be given on a broken plate; for they were *apapātra* (*MS.* X. 51).[2]

In the beginning the *caṇḍālas*, including even the *mṛtapas* and *dombas*, belonged to the Śūdra *varṇa* (Kane 1941: II. I. 166, 168, 184). The sign of breach appears with Pāṇini's *niravasita* Śūdra. In the next phase (maybe not chronologically but in the course of degradation of certain social groups), the *caṇḍālas* were openly condemned. And later it seems that not only with regard to the *caṇḍālas* but some other groups also, which enjoyed a better position previously, there was a general downward movement in the social hierarchy.

For instance, the *niṣādas* were regarded by some as belonging to the Vaiśya *varṇa* (*SKD.* II. 902), and the *rathakāras* (or *ugra*) were *dvijas*, i.e. they belonged to the cluster of the first three *varṇas* (*Comm. on Āps. Dh. Sūt.* p. 111). According to another authority, the *rathakāras* occupied a place somewhere between the Vaiśyas and the Śūdras (Macdonell and Keith 1958: III. 204). Eventually, the two groups went even lower down in the *varṇa* hierarchy. Kauṭilya placed the *niṣādas* among the Śūdras or at a still lower level but not as low as the *caṇḍālas* (*AS*. III. 7). In the *Mahābhārata*, Ekalavya, the son of a *niṣāda* king (or that of a tribal chief?) was denied the privilege of being accepted as a pupil by the Brāhmaṇa Droṇa, because a *niṣāda* could not be instructed along with princes who were usually Kṣatriyas. The story of subsequent sacrifice of Ekalavya and how he was rendered ineffective is too well known to be repeated here. The degradation of the *rathakāras* was already evident (*Baud. Dh. Sūt.* I. 9. 5); in the *Arthaśāstra* they had the same position as that of the *niṣādas*. That is, they (the *rathakāras*) were like the Śūdra but not like the *caṇḍālas* (*AS*. III. 7).

At about this time we notice attempts to fit various extraneous groups into the *varṇa*-structure. Not only positional changes were taking place among various occupational, regional and unspecified groups—hitherto mentioned in one or another texts—but also some more names, 'ficticious' or 'real', needed to be located in the *varṇa*-structure. Therefore, from about 800 B.C. (the approximate time of beginning the composition of the Sūtra literature), the theory of miscegenation (i.e. *varṇa-saṁkara*) was advanced by the Brāhmaṇas to explain the origin of those born out of the mixture of four *varṇas* (Dutt. 1931: I. 227-33). Now the Brāhmaṇa law-givers attempted to explain the parentage of all 'mixed-*varṇa*' children as well as the presence of certain groups according to the four-*varṇa* theory. The law-givers assigned them specified places within or outside the *varṇa* hierarchy, thus creating further subdivisions among the Śūdras, again, vertically.

This step was probably necessitated by innumerable marriages taking place among different *varṇas*, on the one hand, and the felt-need of ranking most of the existing groups in relation to the four *varṇas*, on the other. Because, as time went on, the relationship between the *RV* people and the locals was obviously not confined to the military, political, ritual or economic aspects of life. There was yet another important dimension of their relationship which, unless effectively proscribed, emerged from the occurrence of inter-*varṇa* marriages.

In this context, one notices immediately the significance of inter-*varṇa* marriages, the meaning of which could easily be extended beyond the four *varṇas*. First, therefore, one finds that two types of inter-*varṇa* marriages were classified, namely, the *anuloma* and the *pratiloma*. When a higher *varṇa* man took a lower *varṇa* woman as his wife, it was known as *anuloma* marriage, i.e. hypogamy. Conversely, the marriage of a lower *varṇa* man with a higher *varṇa* woman was known as *pratiloma* marriage, i.e. hypergamy. The society being patriarchial, at least that is what was propagated through literature, hypogamy was tolerated but not encouraged, while hypergamy was unequivocally condemned.[3]

Children born of these two types of marriage derived their names accordingly. That is, they were known as *anuloma* and *pratiloma* children. These children were called the 'mixed-*varṇa*' ones and names were given to each of them, not only to those belonging to the first-order miscegenation but also according to genealogy often involving the second-, third- or the fourth-order miscegenation too. All possible permutation and combination of the four *varṇas* was taken into account that a particular author could think of, and some of the children were absorbed into the existing four *varṇas* while some were not.[4] Those who were excluded formed separate units and their occupations were also specified, especially by Manu.

For a clear appreciation of these efforts of lawgivers, the following Table has been prepared giving the details of the enumerated varieties of primary *anuloma* and *pratiloma* children, and also of some removed by the second or third degree of miscegenation. This will help us in locating some of the units mentioned hitherto. Only those authors are listed in the Table who are considered authoritative by the Hindus, and also the corresponding social groups by indicating significant trends in this context which are relevant to our study. Although a detailed discussion follows later, two lexicons are included in the Table. One is the earliest known and the other the most important.

We shall discuss only those names in the Table which are opposite to our study. But before that let us find out the general attitude of different authors *vis-a-vis* the progenies of inter-*varṇa* marriage. As with the incidence of inter-*varṇa* marriage, the

TABLES OF INTER-VARṆA MARRIAGES AND THEIR PROGENIES

1. PRIMARY ANULOMA SONS

Authority	*Parentage*		*Sons*	
	Father	*Mother*		
1. *Baudhāyana-dharma-sūtra*	Brāhmaṇa	Kṣatriya	Savarṇa	1. 9. 1-5
	Brāhmaṇa	Vaiśya	Ambaṣṭḥa	
	Brāhmaṇa	Śūdra	Pāraśava/Naiṣāda	
	Kṣatriya	Vaiśya	Savarṇa	
	Kṣatriya	Śūdra	Ugra	
	Vaiśya	Śūdra	Rathakāra	
2. *Gautama-dharma-sūtra*	Brāhmaṇa	Kṣatriya	Savarṇa/Mūrdhavāsika	Mitra 1965: 158
	Brāhmaṇa	Vaiśya	Niṣāda/Bhujjya Kanaka	
	Brāhmaṇa	Śūdra	Pāraśava	
	Kṣatriya	Vaiśya	Ambaṣṭha/Māhiṣya	
	Kṣatriya	Śūdra	Dausyanta/Yavana	
	Vaiśya	Śūdra	Ugra/Karaṇa	
3. *Vaikhānasa-smārta-sūtra*	Brāhmaṇa	Kṣatriya	Savarṇa/Nṛpa	Mitra 1965: 158
	Brāhmaṇa	Vaiśya	Ambaṣṭha	
	Brāhmaṇa	Śūdra	Pāraśava	
	Kṣatriya	Vaiśya	Madgu/Mahanarma	
	Kṣatriya	Śūdra	Ugra	
	Vaiśya	Śūdra	Cucaka	

4. *Arthaśāstra of Kauṭilya*	Brāhmaṇa	Kṣatriya	Savarṇa	*AS*. III. 7
	Brāhmaṇa	Vaiśya	Ambaṣṭḥa	*Ibid.*
	Brāhmaṇa	Śūdra	Niṣāda/Pāraśava	*Ibid.*
	Kṣatriya	Vaiśya	Savarṇa	*Ibid.*
	Kṣatriya	Śūdra	Ugra	*Ibid.*
	Vaiśya	Śūdra	Śūdra	*Ibid.*
5. *Śāśvatakośa*	Brāhmaṇa	Kṣatriya	—	
	Brāhmaṇa	Vaiśya	—	
	Brāhmaṇa	Śūdra	—	
	Kṣatriya	Vaiśya	—	
	Kṣatriya	Śūdra	—	
	Vaiśya	Śūdra	Ugra	*SK*. 184
6. *Manusmṛti*	Brāhmaṇa	Kṣatriya	Murdhavāsika	
	Brāhmaṇa	Vaiśya	Ambaṣṭha	*MS*. X. 8
	Brāhmaṇa	Śūdra	Pāraśava/Niṣāda	*Ibid.*
	Kṣatriya	Vaiśya	Māhiṣya	
	Kṣatriya	Śūdra	Ugra	*MS*. X. 9
	Vaiśya	Śūdra	Karaṇa	
7. *Amarakośa*	Brāhmaṇa	Kṣatriya	—	
	Brāhmaṇa	Śūnra	—	*AK*. II 10.2
	Brāhmaṇa	Vaiśya	Ambaṣṭḥa	
	Kṣatriya	Vaiśya	—	
	Kṣatriya	Śūdra	—	
	Vaiśya	Śūdra	—	

Authority	Parentage		Sons	
	Father	Mother		
8. *Vāsiṣṭha-smṛti*	Brāhmaṇa	Kṣatriya	—	*Vāsiṣṭha* XVIII. 8
	Brāhmaṇa	Vaiśya	Ambaṣṭḥa	*Vāsiṣṭha* XVIII. 9
	Brāhmaṇa	Śūdra	Niṣāda	
	Kṣatriya	Vaiśya	—	
	Kṣatriya	Śūdra	—	
	Vaiśya	Śūdra	—	

2. PRIMARY PRATILOMA SONS

Authority	Parentage		Sons	
	Father	Mother		
1. *Baudhāyana-dharma-sūtra*	Śūdra	Brāhmaṇa	Caṇḍāla	I. 9. 6-14
	Śūdra	Kṣatriya	Kṣatta	
	Śūdra	Vaiśya	Māgadha	
	Kṣatriya	Brāhmaṇa	Sūta	
	Kṣatriya	Kṣatriya	Āyogava	
	Kṣatriya	Brāhmaṇa	—	
2. *Gautama-dharma-sūtra*	Śūdra	Brāhmaṇa	—	
	Śūdra	Kṣatriya	Vaidehaka/Pulkaśa	
	Śūdra	Vaiśya	Valdahaka/Āyogava	Mitra 1965: 160
	Vaiśya	Brāhmaṇa	Kṣattrī/Māgadha	
	Vaiśya	Kṣatriya	Māgadha/Dhavira	
	Kṣatriya	Brāhmaṇa	Sūta	
3. *Vaikhānasa-smārta-sūtra*	Śūdra	Brāhmaṇa	Caṇḍāla	
	Śūdra	Kṣatriya	Pulkaśa	Mitra 1965: 161
	Śūdra	Vaiśya	Vaidehaka	
	Vaiśya	Brāhmaṇa	Māgadha	
	Vaiśya	Kṣatriya	Āyogava	
	Kṣatriya	Brāhmaṇa	Sūta	

Authority	Parentage		Sons	
	Father	*Mother*		
4. *Arthaśāstra of Kauṭilya*	Śūdra	Brāhmaṇa	Caṇḍāla	*AS*. II. 7
	Śūdra	Kṣatriya	Kṣatta	*Ibid.*
	Śudra	Vaiśya	Āyogava	*Ibid.*
	Vaiśya	Brāhmaṇa	Vaidehaka	*Ibid.*
	Vaiśya	Kṣatriya	Māgadha	*Ibid.*
	Kṣatriya	Brāhmaṇa	Sūta	*Ibid.*
	Ugra	Kṣatta	Śvapāka	
5. *Sāśvatakośa*	Śūdra	Brāhmaṇa	Caṇḍāla	
	Śūdra	Kṣatriya	Ksattṛī	
	Śūdra	Vaiśya	—	*SK*. 345
	Vaiśya	Brāhmaṇa	Vaidehaka	
	Vaiśya	Kṣatriya	Māgadha	
	Kṣatriya	Brāhmaṇa	Sūta	*SK*. 276
6. *Manusmṛti*	Śūdra	Brāhmaṇa	Caṇḍāla	*MS*. X. 12
	Śūdra	Kṣatriya	Kṣatta	*Ibid.*
	Śūdra	Vaiśya	Āyogava	*Ibid.*
	Vaiśya	Brāhmaṇa	Vaideha	*MS*. X. 11
	Vaiśya	Kṣatriya	Māgadha	*Ibid.*
	Kṣatriya	Brāhmaṇa	Sūta	

7. *Amarakośa*	Śūdra	Brāhmaṇa	Caṇḍāla	*AK*. II. 10.4
	Śūdra	Kṣatriya	Kṣatta	
	Śūdra	Vaiśya	—	
	Vaiśya	Brāhmaṇa	Vaidehaka	*AK*. II. 10.3
	Vaiśya	Kṣatriya	Māgadha	*AK*. II. 10.2
	Kṣatriya	Brāhmaṇa	Sūta	*AK*. II. 10.3
8. *Vāsiṣṭhasmṛti*	Śūdra	Brāhmaṇa	Caṇḍāla	*Vāsiṣṭha XVIII* 1
	Śūdra	Kṣatriya	Vaiṇa	*Vāsiṣṭha* XIII 2
	Śūdra	Vaiśya	Antyavāsayin	*Vāsiṣṭha* XIII 3
	Vaiśya	Brāhmaṇa	Ramaka	*Vāsiṣṭha* XIII 4
	Vaiśya	Kṣatriya	Pulkaśa	*Vāsiṣṭha* XIII 5
	Kṣatriya	Brāhmaṇa	Sūta	

3. FURTHER 'MIXED-VARṆA' SONS

Authority	Parentage		Sons	
	Father	Mother		
1. *Baudhayāna-dharma-sūtra*	Ugra	Kṣattrī	Śvapaca (Ambaṣṭḥa + Brāhmaṇa)	
	Vaiśya	Śūdra	Rathakāra	
2. *Vaikhānasa-smārta-sūtra*	Brāhmaṇa	Brahmaṇa	Nāpita (Adultery)	Mitra 1965: 158, 162
	Caṇḍāla	Brāhmaṇa	Śvapaca	
3. *Arthaśāstra of Kauṭilya*	Ambaṣṭḥa	Vaidehaka	Rathakāra Veṇa	
4. *Manusmṛti*	Kṣatta	Ugra	Śvapaca	Mitra 1965: 158-60, 162

same degree of tolerance or intolerance is noticed with regard to sons born of them. For example, four authorities quoted in the Table concerning *anuloma* children agree that sons born of marriages with the next lower *varṇa* girls (especially those between a Brāhmaṇa man and a Kṣatriya woman) were of the same *varṇa* (that is, as that of the father). The other three made no mention of it. That the *anuloma* sons of the *dvija* parents were included in the four-*varṇa* structure of society (especially those having their mothers from the next lower *varṇa*) is supported by the fact that they were called *savarṇa* (i.e. of the same *varṇa*) sons. Even in the *Manusmṛti* it was only the child of a Brāhmaṇa from a Śūdra woman who was castigated.

Nonetheless, Manu took great care in detailing the names of all the possible six varieties of sons born of such union. But that this form of marriage was not encouraged and, in fact, discouraged indirectly is seen from the shares of patrimony as specified by Kauṭilya and Manu (*AS*. III. 6; *MS*. IX. 153). A son's share of inheritance depended very much on the *varṇa* of his mother, higher the *varṇa* more the share. The son of a Brāhmaṇa man and a Śūdra woman received the minimum share of inheritance. Manu, in fact, opined that the sons of a Śūdra woman having a Brāhmaṇa, Kṣatriya or Vaiśya husband had no claim to patrimony. He should be satisfied with whatever was given to him (*MS*. IX. 155). It seems, however, that marriage among the *dvijas* was not so much discouraged as that between Brāhmaṇa and Śūdra. Even Kauṭilya, who was not supposedly obsessed with *varṇa* superiority, did not allow full inheritance to the son of a Śūdra mother, should he happen to be the only son of a Brāhmaṇa.

More importantly, we find from the Table that in the context of primary *anuloma* sons the authorities disagree on almost each name and parentage. However, without going into a detailed discussion on all the names, we shall select only those with which we are already familiar. Therefore, we shall concentrate on *ugra*, *niṣāda* and *rathakāras* alone, and try to collect whatever information is available about them.

Ugra. As regards an *ugra*, there was the maximum degree of agreement in the sense that five out of eight authors agreed that he was an offspring of a Kṣatriya father and a Śūdra mother.

In the *Manusmṛti*, the *ugras* have been described as a very cruel people living in mountains, forests, under a tree or near crematorium. Manu specified their occupation as that of catching and killing of animals which lived in holes.

Niṣāda. About the parentage of a *niṣāda*, only one author was of the view that he was born of a Brāhmaṇa father and a Śūdra mother. Others either left him out or mentioned different parentage and gave him an alternative name, that of *pāraśava*. To be precise, one author did not mention him at all; another made his mother a Vaiśya (instead of a Śūdra); two other authors mentioned *pāraśava* (with the same parentage as *niṣāda*) but did not mention *niṣāda*; and three authors mentioned both *niṣāda* and *pāraśava*. There is yet another theory about the origin of *niṣāda* where we find that he was born from the thigh of a mythical king whose name was Veṇa. After he was thus born he was asked 'to sit down', and that is how he acquired his name *niṣāda* (*Mbh*. Santi. 59. 101-03). Significantly, Veṇa has been accused by Manu of being the king during whose reign the mixture of *varṇas* took place in a big way (*MS*. IX. 66-67). Still a *niṣāda/pāraśava* was an *anuloma* son who remained within the four *varṇas* of Hindu society, and was accepted socially and legally. Both Kauṭilya and Manu discussed his inheritance of patrimony, his shares declining from one to the other (*AS*. III. 6; *MS*. IX. 153).

Rathakāra. Only one out of eight authorities mentioned this group as having Vaiśya fathers and Śūdra mothers. According to another authority, this group comprised second-order *anuloma* sons. Their fathers were supposed to be *māhiṣya* (born of Kṣatriya father and Vaiśya mother) and mothers *karaṇa* (born of Vaiśya father and Śūdra mother).

But Kauṭilya treated the *rathakāras* separately as an occupational group belonging to the Śūdra *varṇa* or lower than that but not to *caṇḍālas* (*AS*. III. 7). Further, the parentage of a *rathakāra* is described in the *Arthaśāstra* as that the father was an *ambaṣṭha* (i.e. one born of a Brāhmaṇa father and Vaiśya mother) and mother a *vaidehaka* who is born of a Vaiśya father and Brāhmaṇa mother (*AS*. III. 7). This shows that a *rathakāra* is second-order 'mixed-*varṇa*' son having an *anuloma* father and a *pratiloma* mother. Kauṭilya further stated that by profession a *vaiṇa/vaiṇya* also was known as a *rathakāra*.

To the *pratiloma* sons, however, the authorities were not at all sympathetic. In the Table we find that not all the possible six varieties of sons were enumerated by the eight authors. Only four of them did and even among them there was disagreement regarding names and parentage of children. However, the enumerated varieties of sons are arranged below, according to the order of agreement among the authors about their parentage. As in the case of *anuloma* sons, here also we shall mention only those that are relevant to us.

Sūta. Seven out of eight authors agreed about *sūta's* parentage. One who disagreed made his father a Vaiśya instead of a Kṣatriya. A *sūta* was a court official. In earlier times, he used to participate in horse-sacrifice, and also looked after horses (*Kāty*. *Śr*. *Sūt*. II. 1.15). Therefore, he was mentioned as a driver (of chariots?), groom and also as a bard. According to Manu, he was a groom (*MS*. X. 47). A *sūta* was also mentioned as one of the eleven *ratnins* (i.e. jewels) in the court of a king and as one of eight *vīras*, who eagerly awaited the arrival of a king and followed him (Dutt 1931: 165; *Bṛ*. *Ār*. *Up*. IV. 3. 289.37, 290.38). The sons of *sūtas* belonging to Kāśī and Videha were brave warriors. The respectability of a *sūta* is further evident by the stipulation that food offered by him could be taken by all.

Caṇḍāla/Śvapaca. Since *caṇḍālas* and/or *śvapacas* have often been bracketed together, it is better to treat them as synonymous, although their attributed parentage was different. A *śvapaca* was born of an *ugra* father and *kṣatta* mother. Since he was born of an *anuloma* father and *pratiloma* mother, a *śvapaca* was supposedly lower than a *caṇḍāla* who was primarily a *pratiloma*. The occupation of *śvapacas*, as pointed out earlier, was connected with dogs. About *caṇḍālas* we only know that sometimes they were employed by a king; that they lived outside the village and had little contact with it. In any case, the *caṇḍālas* and *śvapacas* had earned the displeasure of all the authorities.

Kṣatta (var. Lect. *Kṣattu/Kṣatṛ/kṣattṛ/Kṣattra/Kṣattare/Kṣattri*).

He was mentioned by seven out of eight authors. Among them five disagreed, one agreed and two remained silent about *kṣatta*'s parentage. There were court officials who were designated as *kṣatra* (Dattaray 1962). Once *kṣatta* is cited as participating in horse-sacrifice, but by profession he was an accountant and councillor of a king. Afterwards we find *kṣattas* being mentioned as door-keepers, messengers, or drivers (*sārathi*) according to *Amarakośa* (*AK.* II. 8.59). Manu assigned to them the double role of grooming (of horses) as well as of catching and killing of animals which lived in holes (*MS.* X. 49).

Māgadha. Four authors agreed about his parentage, two differed while agreeing between themselves, one disagreed from all, and one remained completely silent. For *māgadhas* two occupations were prescribed. Supposedly they lived on 'words' (*vākya-jīvin*), i.e. as story-tellers, bards, court-poets and, also, as traders (*MS.* X. 47).

Vaidehaka/Vaideha. Four authors agreed on parentage of a *vaidehaka*, two disagreed from the four but agreed between themselves, and the remaining two were silent. Two occupations were mentioned for a *vaidehaka*, and there was a general agreement about them. He could either be a trader (*AS.* III. 4.25) or a harem attendant (*MS.* X. 47).

Āyogava. About an *āyogava* there was the least agreement among the authors. Four of them agreed on his parentage while one among them equated him to a *vaidehaka*, one disagreed and the other three remained silent. He was mentioned as a wood-curver (*MS.* X. 48).

The foregoing description of the *pratiloma* sons reveals at a glance a good deal of overlapping of occupations. For instance, *kṣatta* and *sūta* had the common job of a driver (of chariots?), and were also connected with horse-sacrifice; *māgadha* and *sūta* were bards while *māgadha* and *vaidehaka* were traders. From the nature of occupations assigned to them, mutual distance among the *pratiloma* sons is noticed not only with respect to multiplicity of jobs they were supposed to perform but also their proximity or distance from the established political authority and social organization.

The roles of *sūta* and *kṣatta* were important. Not only a large number of jobs were performed by them but they were also connected with a king's court, serving him as important officials. The *sūtas* were well known for their bravery, and they adorned the court of a king. Moreover, their social ranking is noted from the fact that their food was accepted by all. A *kṣatta*, although a *pratiloma* son, was equated to an *anuloma* one and was assigned the role of catching and killing the animals that lived in holes. Next in order, a *māgadha* could be associated with the court in his role as a court poet. Also, a *vaidehaka* lived within a royal household because of his duty as a harem-attendant (see Lassen 1847. I. 819).

It was only the *āyogavas* who appeared to have nothing to do either with a royal family or a king's court. As a wood-curver, he not only followed a single profession but an independent one as well. The latter fact is again underlined by the other interpretation that an *āyagu* was a woman 'independently selecting her husband'.

The positions of the *caṇḍālas* and the *śvapacas* are seen to be farthest away from the established political authority and the extant social organization. The *śvapacas* were connected all along with dogs alone, and the habitats of the *caṇḍālas* nearest to civilization was on the outskirt of settled villages. Their occupations did not come in conflict with others; it was not needed for them to be physically present before or near a king, although they could have been in his employ.

Significantly, almost all the *pratiloma* sons, except the *caṇḍālas*, had some specified, although duplicate, occupations, often better than those of the Śūdras who were assigned a general and the degrading job like that of serving the *dvijas* alone. Nonetheless, the *pratiloma* sons were placed outside the four-*varṇa* system, obviously lower in hierarchy than the Śūdras. Even the *pratiloma* sons of *dvijas* were no exceptions in this respect as they were segregated too, both occupationally and *varṇa*-wise. For instance, although *māgadhas* and *vaidehakas* could have been included in the Vaiśya *varṇa* according to their profession, they were earlier Śūdras and afterwards placed even lower in *varṇa* hierarchy (*AS*. III. 7; *SKD*. I. 55).

In this respect, it is also to be noted that a *caṇḍāla*, although a primary *pratiloma* son, was condemned in no uncertain terms. In fact, some other 'mixed-*varṇa*' sons belonging to the second- or third-order like the *rathakāra* of the *Arthaśāstra* or *kaivarta* (fishermen, boatmen) of the *Manusmṛti* were not treated so contemptuously and were ranked higher than the *caṇḍālas*.

Possibly, because of such divergence of opinions, the theory of 'mixed-*varṇa*' children has often been questioned and considered a 'fiction' (Sharma 1980: 240, 335-36). However, if 'mixed-*varṇa*' marriages are accepted, which was not questioned by anyone and which undoubtedly did take place in society, then the existence of 'mixed-*varṇa*' children cannot be denied. One may point out that not only the liturgical texts but even the *Arthaśātra* with a penchant for realistic description followed the same pattern in so far as the 'mixed-*varṇa*' children were concerned. This could have been possible only with the existence of such children in society. Furthermore, the general agreement on the names of such children (although not always on their parentage) and their occurrence in the Brāhmaṇical literature are so widespread that it is difficult to dismiss the incidence of 'mixed-*varṇa*' children as a 'fiction'/'fraud' without any valid alternative. Probably, their names, especially of the progenies of successive orders of inter-*varṇa* marriages, were borrowed from the existing social groups, who had to be assimilitated into the current social structure. In this context, occupational and territorial names like *niṣāda*, *rathakāra*, *sūta*, *ugra*, *māgadha*, *vaidehaka* and *āyogava* are suggestive of their prior existence. While devising their parentage, occupation, etc. and carrying the paradigm to an absurd length, the Brāhmaṇical ingenuity had its full play.

Another set of literature that followed the same theory of miscegenation, strengthening thereby the above surmise, is the Sanskrit dictionaries. These lexicons, admittedly, were not altogether free from the Brāhmaṇical bias. But since they were not written primarily from a didactic point of view but from that of enumeration and explanation of different words and terms, the information contained in them may be more reliable if selected judiciously. The dictionaries supplied, in addition, more detailed information about those beyond the four *varṇas*, i.e. the forest-dwellers, several occupational groups, the 'mixed-*varṇa*' sons, etc.

Most of these social groupings, some time or other, were equated to *caṇḍāla*, the lowest group in the social hierarchy. The dictionaries described their occupations, and also their eventual categorization.

Four lexicons have been selected, the earliest one and the other three containing not only significant information regarding the *caṇḍālas* and about the *pratilomas*, but also registering an evolutionary trend in the course of categorization of social groups beyond the four *varṇas*. The dictionaries are arranged chronologically covering a period of nearly 2,000 years. Our inquiry begins with *caṇḍālas*, because this was one of the oldest groups that existed in ancient times and is still identifiable in some places of India. Those who formed this group were and still are supposed to be 'untouchable'. A search for this particular group and other synonymous units as given in the lexicons may, therefore, make the task of identification of 'untouchables' easier.[5]

The earliest dictionary, the *Śāśvatakośa*, also known as *Anekārtha-samuchhaya* (henceforth abbreviated as *SK*), is supposed to be the oldest homonymous extant Sanskrit dictionary (Macdonell 1962: 368; Zachariae 1897: 24). Names of eight groups are found in this, which are equated to (and/or placed coterminally with) the *caṇḍālas* directly or indirectly. The enumerated groups are *antavāsayin*, *caṇḍāla*, *nāpita*, *jananggama*, *divākīrti*, *plava*, *mātaṅga* and *śvapaca* (*SK*. 482, 277, 737, 611).

The second lexicon, the *Amarakośa* (abbreviated as *AK*), was composed not later than the sixth century A.D. As a complete Sanskrit dictionary this is probably the oldest and the most important one (Kosambi 1955: 57; Macdonell 1962: 368; Zachariae 1897: 11). A set of ten groups is identified in the *AK*, one of which is explained by four other names. The ten groups are: *caṇḍāla*, *plava*, *mātaṅga*, *divākīrti*, *jananggama*, *niṣāda*, *śvapaca*, *antevāsin*,[6] *caṇḍāla* and *pukkasa* (*AK*. II. 10. 19-20). The group of *divākīrti* is further subdivided into *kṣurin*, *muṇḍiṇ*, *nāpita* and *antevāsin* (*AK*. II. 10.10). Noticeably, five new names are added in the *AK*, viz. *niṣāda*, *pukkasa*, *antevāsin*, *kṣuriṇ* and *muṇḍiṇ*. Another group of people—*kirāta*, *śabara* and *pulinda*, commonly known as *mlechha*—is also equated to *caṇḍāla* (*AK*. II. 10.20).

The *Halāyudhakośa*, also known as *Abhidhānaratnamālā* (henceforth to be referred as *HK*) reveals an attempt to bring about an order in an otherwise chaotic situation. The *HK* belongs to the early or the later part of the tenth century A.D. (Macdonell 1962: 368; Zachariae 1897: 26) and is the best synonymous dictionary in Sanskrit. Here two categories are mentioned, known as those of *caṇḍāla* and *antajāti*, in which altogether sixteen names are listed.

As synonymous with *caṇḍāla*, it mentions: *antavāsayin*, *caṇḍāla*, *niṣāda*, *jananggama*, *śvapaca*, *pukkasa*, *mātaṅga* and *plavaka*, and the authority of the Smṛtis is cited to strengthen it (*HK*. 598). Instead of *antevāsin* of the *AK*, we have *antavāsayin* here, which is included under *divākīrti* in the *AK*, but is absent in the *HK*. Elsewhere, however, *divākīrti* is equated to *kṣuramardin*, *caṇḍila* (var. lact. *caṇḍāla*?) and *nāpita* (*HK*. 289, 814), which indicates that the same occupational group of barber is present here also. People forming the *mlechha* group and belonging to the special type of *caṇḍāla* in the *AK*., viz. *kirāta*, *śabara* and *pulinda*, are also *mlechha* in the *HK*. But they form a separate category and are called *antajāti*, and their number is increased by five more names: *nistya*, *nahala*, *bhaṭa*, *māla*, and *bhīlla* (*HK*. 599). Thus, the two categories of *caṇḍāla* and *antajāti* in the *HK* contain sixteen groups, eight under each.

The last lexicon, the *Śabdakalpadruma* (*SKD*) was compiled in 1845. This lexicon is precise, systematic, updated and has the additional advantage of drawing upon other sources whenever necessary. As to the categorization of the *caṇḍāla* and other groups and also in their enumeration, the *SKD* reveals significant facts.

We have already remarked how the *HK* includes eight groups headed by *antyavāsayin* under the category of *caṇḍāla* and other eight under that of *antajāti*. The *SKD* similarly arranges, but more efficiently and precisely, fourteen groups under two categories of *antyaja* and *antyavāsayin*, seven under each. It thus reduces the number from sixteen of *HK* to fourteen. The *antyaja* category is equated to the Śūdra, and, according to Yama, it contains seven *jātis* belonging to the 'washermen/dyer' category (*rajakādi saptajatayoḥ*) namely, *rajaka*, *carmakāra* (leather worker), *nata* (actor/dancer), *barudha*, *kaivarta* (boatmen/fishermen), *meda* and *bhīlla* (*SKD*. I. 55; IV. 275).

The *antyavāsayin* category, on the other hand, deals with the *caṇḍāla* proper and other synonymous groups, as is evident from the phrase *caṇḍālādi saptajātayoḥ* (*SKD*. I. 55). Āṅgiras is quoted in this context and the group of *antyavāsayin* is found to contain the same number of seven *jātis*, namely, *caṇḍāla*, *śvapaca*, *kṣatta*, *sūta*, *vaidehaka*, *māgadha* and *āyogava* (*ibid.*)

The evidence from the four dictionaries shows that all these people who are made synonymous or homonymous with *caṇḍālas* may be classified under three categories of social groups or clusters of categories, each category containing several social groups:

(1) *Mlechha* is a generic term denoting *kirāta*, *śabara* and *pulinda* who are treated as *caṇḍāla* in the *AK*. In the *HK* five more names are added to it, and the group is referred to as *antajāti*, separated from that of the *caṇḍālas*. To all appearances the *mlechhas* seem to consist solely of forest-dwellers or of the so-called 'tribes'. At least four out of eight groups enumerated under this category in the *HK*, i.e. the *kirāta*, *śabara*, *pulinda* and *bhīla*, are designated as tribes in later literature.

(2) The second category is occupational, the oldest being that of the barbers. The identification of barbers with *caṇḍāla* is clearly recorded in the *SK*, *AK* and *HK*. But from the *HK* onward they are dropped out from the group of *caṇḍālas* and are not included either in the *antyaja* or the *antyavāsayin* category of the *SKD*. Nonetheless, they lend one of their names (i.e. *antyavāsayin*) to the lowest category, that is, the untouchables. The next cluster forming an occupational group is composed of fishermen. Their names are *kaivarta*, *dāsa* and *dhīvara*, which are probably synonymous and are first enumerated in the *AK* and is followed by *HK*, although never equated to *caṇḍāla*. But the other two names, i.e. *jananggama* and *plava/plavaka*, which are connected with water and probably could have belonged to the fishermen category, are synonymous with *caṇḍāla* from the earliest lexicon, i.e. the *SK*.

In the *SKD* the occupational group, also not equated to *caṇḍāla*, is indicated by *antyaja*. This category is formed by including some of the above and several other new ones. For instance, *kaivarta* from the *AK* and *HK* belonging to the fishermen category and *bhīlla* from the *mlechha* group (of the *HK* alone) are placed together with *rajaka*, *carmakāra*, *nata*, *barudha* and *meda*.

(3) The *caṇḍāla* category (or *antyavāsayin* for that matter) contains 'mixed-*varṇa*' children and that again *pratiloma* sons only with unidentified occupations, at least not clear from their names. It may be pointed out here that, out of seven, only *caṇḍāla* and

śvapaca are the old and regular names, while others are found in the *SK*, *AK*, and *HK* but not as synonymous with *caṇḍālas* (*SK*, 276, 321, 316, 346; *HK*. 435, 449, 571). None of them, however mentions *āyogava*. The names equivalent with *caṇḍālas*, present in early lexicons but absent from the final enumeration, are *mātaṅga* and *pukkasa/pakkasa*. However, in other literature (e.g. in the *Mahābhārata* and *Daśa-kumāra-carita*) *mātaṅga* is found synonymous with *caṇḍāla*. The *caṇḍāla* and *śvapaca*, along with *mātaṅga*, have often been used synonymously, that is, one standing for the other. In the story of Viśvāmitra and *caṇḍāla*, we find the latter being mentioned ten times as *śvapaca*, eight times as *caṇḍāla* and twice as *mātaṅga*.

The three lexicons, that is, the *AK*, *HK* and *SKD*, contain information which may be considered as landmarks in the history of *caṇḍālas* in ancient India. Previously, in the *SK* and more elaborately in the *AK*, it was more of an enumeration and listing of *caṇḍālas* and similar group than anything else. It was first in the *HK* that an attempt was made to clarify the confusing situation regarding *caṇḍālas* and their synonyms. In the process, two mutually exclusive categories emerged, one comprising what appears to be the forest-dwellers or tribal people mainly and the other—possibly the lowest—*caṇḍālas* and their equivalents. As to the principle underlying this division, whatever else may be the basis of it, occupation does not appear to be the guiding factor. While the *caṇḍāla* category contains almost all the previously known groups, that of *antajāti* includes several new names of unknown occupation and origin, among which a preponderence of tribal names (at least which became so later on) does not escape our attention.

Later in the *SKD*, in spite of superficial similarity in the names and number of groups under each category, the basis of characterization was not the same as in the *HK*. The *antajāti* category of the *HK* possibly assumed the name of *antyaja* in the *SKD* and enlisted more functional groups, leaving aside the tribal ones completely. Some of the groups belonging to the *antyaja* category have eponymous caste identifications like *rajaka*, *carmakāra*, etc. Significantly, most of them (i.e. people belonging to this category) have such occupations that needed constant interaction with other *varṇas* in society. Apparently, this time the factor of occupation was taken into account.

The *antyavasāyin* category, on the other hand, contains those names which were given to the children of *pratiloma* marriages and *śvapacas*. An examination of its membership shows the presence of an overwhelming number of *pratiloma* progenies and the corresponding absence of other constituents hitherto present in all other lexicons. The occupations of *pratiloma* sons are not clear from their names, and even when they were made so, there was hardly any explanation to justify their lower position than some of those belonging to the *antyaja* category. One may also point out here the *niṣādas* whose position is very significant. From its elevated position in the Vedic literature, it came down to the level of the lowest in the social hierarchy. This happened around *ca.* fourth century A.D. But from the *HK* onward (i.e. from about the tenth century A.D.) the *niṣādas* disappeared from the list of either *antyaja* or *antyavāsayin.*

Apart from their socio-economic relevance to society, these two clear-cut divisions have also been spiritually well fortified in the *SKD*. The names of sages and *śāstras* are quoted to strengthen their authenticity and antiquity. The *antyaja* category seems to have been already familiar in society, since it was authorized by the Smṛtis and sanctioned by lawgivers like Atri, Yama, etc. (*Atrisaṁhitā* 199; *Yamasmṛti* 33). The category of *antyavāsayin*, on the other hand, cannot boast of a hoary past or antiquity sanctioned by religion like that of *antyaja.* It has only one sage, i.e. Āṅgirasa, as its patron. And even that is not to be found in the extant *Āṅgirasasmṛti.*[7]

Significantly, the dictionaries reveal three distinct categories which can be placed vertically. The tribal category is one which appears to have remained outside of a close contact with the *varṇa* society as the tribals supposedly lived in forests and mountains. Probably because of that they were omitted from the final enumeration in the *SKD*. The occupational category had three sub-divisions, namely, those of (*a*) barbers, (*b*) fishermen and (*c*) washermen/dyers. All these people, noticeably, had to interact with the *varṇa* society in one way or another. Similarly, almost all the seven castes belonging to the *antyaja* category in the *SKD* rendered some kind of services to the caste Hindus. That way the status of the *antyaja* category was higher than that of the *antyavāsayin* category, which is supported by the fact that it received sanctions from the lawgivers. Thus, the last and the lowest category was that of the unwelcome *antyavāsayin* or *caṇḍālas*, who formed a rather undefined mass but was described mainly as breaking the prevailing marriage norms. The relationship of this category with the *varṇa* society was kept suspended, while its lowest position in society received no scriptural backing.

Furthermore, the lexicons show a gradual increase in the number and importance of 'mixed-*varṇa*' children forming the *caṇḍāla* category. In the final categorization of the *SKD*, the 'mixed-*varṇa*' children monopolized the situation, their number increasing to seven. One, however, must not fail to point out here that with regard to all *pratiloma* sons, mentioned in the *SKD*, there was no unanimity among the different authors cited before as to their names, parentage or occupations, except that *śvapacas* were connected with dogs.

What, however, is not clear is why the *sūtas*, *māgadhas*, *vaidehakas* and *āyogavas* lost their erstwhile prestigious and independent status in society. A *sūta* while following almost similar occupations like those of *kṣattṛ* was downgraded as a *caṇḍāla*. In some respects, *sūta* enjoyed a better position in the sense that he was closely linked up with the court and also had the reputation of being a brave warrior. Similarly, from being traders, the *māgadhas* and *vaidehakas* now became the same as *caṇḍālas*. One may probably explain their downward movement in the social hierarchy from the antipathy to the traders from the time of the *RV*. And possibly the other job of a *vaidehaka* as a harem-attendant was not a very honourable one either. For the *āyogavas*, again, it is hard to account for their degradation unless one accepts the explanation of an *āyogava* being descended from an 'independent' woman or one belonging to a matriarchal tribe. In any case, now all of them were reduced to the category of *caṇḍālas*.

More importantly, the inclusion of all *pratiloma* sons under the category of *caṇḍāla* seems to be an exaggeration. This was done possibly to discourage such misalliances in society. Although the *pratiloma* sons were put into the category of *caṇḍālas*, none of them, except the *caṇḍālas*, was treated as untouchable. The relevant word about untouchable is *aspṛśya*, that is, not to be touched. Although the word *sparśa* (i.e. touch) had been used in connection with *caṇḍālas* and others, the person became pure after a bath or penance even after touching a *caṇḍāla*. But it was in the *Vaikhāna-smārta-sūtra* (belonging to *ca.* fourth century A.D.) that a *caṇḍāla* was ordered to be killed if he entered a village after midday (X. 14). Bāṇabhatta in *Kādambarī* (seventh/eight century A.D.) indicated the untouchable aspect of *caṇḍālas*. As late as in the tenth century A.D., Medhātithi considered only the *caṇḍālas* as untouchables and not others (*MS.* X. 3; Sharma 1980: 291). The *Arthaśāstra*, belonging to the fourth century B.C., noted the degradation, segregation and impurity of the *caṇḍālas* and *śvapacas*, and Manu, belonging to *ca.* second/fourth century A.D. emphasized their total exclusion from the *varṇa* society.

The *caṇḍālas* were the lowest and the worst of all human beings (*Jāt.* 498; *MS.* X. 16, 26). Strong hatred for them is expressed not only by the Brāhmaṇas but in the *Jātakas* as well. For instance, the sight of *caṇḍāla* was inauspicious (*Jāt.* 377), and daughters of a *śreṣṭhi* and priest washed their eyes after having accidentally seen a *caṇḍāla* because he was not fit to be seen (*Jāt.* 498). They were considered low by caste, and two *caṇḍāla* boys lamented over the blemish and inferiority of their caste (*Jāt.* 498). A disciple was ashamed to acknowledge publicly his teacher who was a *caṇḍāla* (*Jāt.* 474). At the same time we find learned *caṇḍālas* (*Jāt.* 497), and when they became Buddhist monks they were treated as equals, for monks have no caste (*Jāt.* 487).

We are not definite, at least not from the *Jātakas* or the *Arthaśāstra*, whether the *caṇḍālas* had to announce their entry into a village so that others could avoid touching them. When the daughters of the *śreṣṭhīs* and priest were passing, the *caṇḍāla* stood at the one side of the road to make room for them. Nevertheless, the *caṇḍālas* were probably known by their dresses, otherwise the daughters could not have recognized them as such. However, the segregation and untouchability of *caṇḍālas* are definitely known by the fifth century A.D., when they had to announce their entry into a village.

Chapter 3

LIFE AND LIVING OF THE UNTOUCHABLES

SO FAR we have cited evidence regarding social groups beyond the four *varṇas* mainly from liturgical and technical literature. Now we shall consult other types of literature to see whether the descriptions of some of these groups provide additional information on their *varṇa* affiliation, socio-economic and ritual status, and other relevant aspects of their life and living. One often finds more of actual conditions existing in society from anecdotes, etc. in descriptive literature than from what is prescribed in didactic texts.

Here we shall examine the life and mode of living of these people. The texts contain sporadic notices concerning the physical characteristics, dwelling places, occupations, nature, habits, dresses, language, etc. of some of these people. From such information it is possible to form a picture of their status in society.

We have so far been concerned with those people who lived on the outskirt of a village, near crematorium, in forests adjoining two or more kingdoms, mountains, etc. which were probable habitats of the untouchables. Among such people, as we have already noted, were the *niṣādas*, *kirātas*, *śabaras*, *pulindas*, *ātavikas*, *lubdhakas*, *mātaṅgas*, *caṇḍālas*, *śvaganins*, *śvapacas*, etc. Of them, we would concentrate particularly on *caṇḍālas* and *śvapacas* as they were condemned by all.

The probable dwelling place and the respectable status of the *niṣādas* have already been discussed. Physically they were dark, had short limbs and red eyes (*SKD*. I. 902). According to some authorities, the *niṣādas* were hunters; and, according to others, fishermen (*Nir*. III. 8.9; *MS*. X. 48; *SKD*. I. 902.). From the story of the 'virtuous hunter' (*dharma-vyādha*) in the *Mahābhārata* we learn some significant facts about the *niṣādas* in particular and the four *varṇas* in general. Here we find that a hunter, a *niṣāda*, was a meat-seller. Nevertheless, the 'virtuous hunter' identified himself as a Śūdra, although as a *niṣāda* he should have been either a 'mixed-*varṇa*' child or a *caṇḍāla*. But in the *Mahābhārata* he is mentioned as a hunter only and not by any other term. It is stated that, because of committing a heinous crime in the former birth (when as a Brāhmaṇa he inadvertently killed a sage), he was cursed to be reborn as a Śūdra, although for a much lesser crime we have noticed a Brāhmaṇa being condemned to be born as a *caṇḍāla*.

The anecdote describes the encounter between the hunter and a learned Brāhmaṇa. Kauśika was an insolent Brāhmaṇa who was proud of his superior birth and wisdom. After chiding him strongly for his arrogance, a chaste woman (*satī*) advised him to go to a hunter (obviously much lower in the *varṇa* hierarchy) and receive instructions from him. The hunter had a beautiful house in Mithilā where Kauśika unhesitatingly (curiously, maybe?) went to receive true knowledge from him.

The 'virtuous hunter', was well versed in philosophy, religion, ethics, etc. and was also pragmatic in his attitude. He told Kauśika that because of his deeds in the former birth he was following in this birth what was his preordained destiny. Since he was born a Śūdra and since one should stick to the vocation of one's family (*kuladharma*), he was performing what his duty was. Serving his parents was the highest of all his duties. He always told the truth, was never envious of anyone, did good to his friends and foes alike, never blamed anyone, practised charities as much as possible, and ate after feeding guests and servants. The hunter scrupulously performed his duties, because deeds were followed by retribution.

Then he listed the general virtues which should be practised by all. One should make a gift of food, do good to others, be kind to all animate creatures, be tolerant and calm, do whatever is just, and be truthful and not greedy because greed leads to sin. He again emphasized that one should stick to one's calling, and not leave it willingly and take up another profession because of other's success or frustration with one's own failures.

By way of justifying his own work, he repeated his earlier arguments that he did not think his calling (i.e. killing animals) was contemptible because that was his duty (*dharma*); and whoever did his own work was virtuous. He informed Kauśika further that he himself did not kill animals but only sold their meat after they had been killed by others.

Then he criticized the doctrine of non-violence.[1] According to him, non-violence was meaningless and contained an inherent fallacy in it. The advice to be non-violent was given without properly understanding the state of things in the world. No one was non-violent in this world because violence was necessary for survival. Animals ate each other, and human beings also unknowingly killed other animals often. 'Tell me', the hunter asked the Brāhmaṇa, 'do not water, trees and earth contain creatures whose life we constantly destroy so that we may live? We kill animals for their flesh and we do the same with trees, creepers, and plants.' Then he cited the examples of men who were famous for their virtues and piety, and yet indulged in killing animals for food. Two thousand cows were cooked daily in the kitchen of king Rantideva, who by giving away that meat with rice attained eternal fame. Moreover, hunting (*mṛgayā*) was an age-old sport for kings, recommended in all religious texts, which involved killing animals in a big way.

Killing of animals was justified from another standpoint. Since animals were offered in sacrifice, they not only went to heaven but by offering their meat for nourishment they did their duty. The killer also performed his duty, because the meat was offered to the gods and manes, and then to the guests and family members. Thus, the act was spiritually beneficial both for the killer and the killed. The Śrutis (Vedas) also stated that plants, creepers, animals and fowls were meant for human consumption. Probably, realizing that he was arguing against non-violence which must have exercised considerable influence on society, the hunter opined that the world was full of contradictory acts. Therefore, the safest was to follow one's own duty.

One may note here that the hunter was a pragmatist as well as a conformist which is evident not only from his apology for violence but from his concept of human duty as well. He thought that the best way to perform one's duty was to follow the hereditary occupations, practise charity and obey the parents.

Having been thus enlightened by the hunter, Kauśika asked him what he should do. He was told by the hunter that all his religious merits were in vain as he left his home to study the

Vedas without obtaining his parents' permission. Therefore, he should go back and serve his parents because that was one's highest duty. Whereupon Kauśika left the hunter, and started for his home (*Mbh*. III. Ch. 127-206).

The foregoing anecdote reveals the anomalous *varṇa* affiliation of a hunter, his material status in the sense that he lived well (not in a 'reserved' area) and the percolated values he upheld. But, in order to find the untouchables, we shall have to look elsewhere for the 'ghettos' and identify them as living there.

The most exhaustive description about the *mātaṅgas*, *caṇḍālas* and *śabaras* is to be found in stories, dramas, etc. where their dwelling place, dress, food, occupation, nature, physical characteristics, etc. are depicted in some detail. The Vindhya forest is mentioned as the dwelling place for the *kirātas*, *śabaras*, *pulindas*, *caṇḍālas* and *mātaṅgas*. Once upon a time the people living there were referred to as *kirātas* only. The name of the son of a *pulinda* was Mātaṅga who seems to have been their leader. The same source also reveals the presence of several Brāhmaṇas among them, because they accepted cooked rice from the *pulindas* which probably degraded them to the same status. These Brāhmaṇas gave up the study of the Vedas, pious and upright life befitting a Brāhmaṇa, and took to the life of the *kirātas* instead. Therefore, in that secluded, fearful and dense forest infested with wild beasts lived the *kirātas* and those 'fallen Brāhmaṇas'. Mātaṅga, their leader, roamed the forest, cruel and arrogant (*Daśa*. II). From the *Jātaka* also we learn that 16,000 Brāhmaṇas had to leave their own country and go to *medya deśa* (*madhya* or *mlechha deśa*?), because they took leftover food from the *caṇḍālas* (*Jāt*. 497).

In the *Kādambarī* there is a graphic description of the *śabaras* whose leader was also known as Mātaṅga. The forest devoid of other human beings was their kingdom where they lived with ferocious tigers. To them, braying of jackals was like chanting the religious texts. They were familiar with dogs, and an owl was their adviser. Harmful bow was their companion, and arrows like poisonous snakes their helpers. Their sole knowledge was their ability to decide about hunting from birds' noise, their song merely a sound to decoy stupid deers. Their religion was to offer human flesh to the goddess Kālī and to worship god with animal blood.

Killing of animals was their sport, meat and alcohol their food and drinking liquor their festival (*Kādam.* Kathāmukham of Pūrvabhāga).

The *kirātas*, according to the Greek sources, lived in the middle of India (McCrindle 1973: 15-16) and the *śvapacas* in mountains extending as far as the Indus (*ibid.*, 22). The *śvapacas* lived in steep, pathless and inaccessible mountaineous regions, and, therefore, they could not be conquered (*ibid.*, 24). According to the Hindu sources, however, the *kirātas* lived in or were connected with mountains.

Kauṭilya mentioned the *śabaras*, *pulindas*, *caṇḍālas* and other 'forest-roamers' (*araṇyacara*) together, and asked the *caṇḍālas* to live near a crematorium (*AS.* II. 4). The *svaganins*, however, were privileged to occupy the outermost ring of the circle in a cantonment (*AS.* I. 1). From the *MS* it appears that all *pratiloma* sons lived near crematorium, mountains, groves, etc. except the *caṇḍālas* and *śvapacas* who lived outside the village (*MS.* X. 50-51).

In the story of Viśvāmitra and *caṇḍāla* we find the *caṇḍālas* living in a forest. It was a known *caṇḍāla* hamlet as Viśvāmitra went there unerringly in search of food during famine. Broken pitchers, clothes and garlands of corpses were scattered everywhere. There were weapons for skinning off dead dogs, and bones and skeletons of pigs and donkeys were lying all around. Snakes' skins were hanging from small huts, and temples had iron bells. The *caṇḍālas* were quarrelling loudly, dogs were roaming around, donkeys kept on braying, hens cackling and owls hooting. (*Mbh.* XII. 139).

After hearing the purpose of Viśvāmitra's visit, a *caṇḍāla* told him that they were not entitled to *dharma* by which he probably implied that there should be no communication between a Brāhmaṇa and *caṇḍāla.* Furthermore, according to the *caṇḍāla*, a Brāhmaṇa must not eat the flesh of a dog. But from another account[2] it seems that Viśvāmitra did steal the hind leg of a dead dog; and, only when he offered it to gods before eating, he was stopped from it by the timely arrival of a deity (*ibid.*).

When Triśaṅku was turned into a *caṇḍāla*, he took a frightful appearance, his skin blue, hair short and rough. Strong physique, body hard as steel, dark complexion, ungainly and cruel appearance have been associated with *caṇḍālas* more than once (*Rām.*

Vāla. 57-60; *Mbh.* Śānti. 139; *Kādam.* Kathāmukham of Pūrvabhāga; *Daśa.* II). Their leader was compared with Ekalavya which indicated his proficiency in archery (*Kādam.* Kathāmukham of Pūrvabhāga), who had red and hard eyes (*Daśa.* II), wide forehead and chest, sharp nose (*Kādam.* Kathāmukham of Pūrvabhāga), and marks of weapons on his body (*Daśa.* II) showing him as a great warrior. Curiously enough, the leader was wearing sacred thread, and, was, therefore, mistaken for a *vipra*, i.e. a Brāhmaṇa (*ibid.*).

The Greek sources described the *śvapacas* and *kirātas* as just and harmless people (McCrindle 1973: 16, 22). The *śvapacas*, according to the Greek sources, were the most advanced of all those living in the periphery. Among them division in society was present as evident from their dresses. There were skilled workers among them as they could construct rafts and manufacture iron implements. They were apparently peace loving, and they maintained friendly relation with others through trade (*ibid.* 24-25). According to the Hindu sources, however, the *śvapacas* were violent and ferocious, and the *mātaṅgas* were of cruel nature too. The *śabaras* were deluded, cruel, vice incarnate, of reproachable conduct (*Kādam.* Kathāmukham of Pūrvabhāga), and had no experience of serving a king (*ibid.*).

The *śvapacas* were dressed in animal hide and the rich among them in cotton garments (McCrindle 1973: 24-25). The *śabaras* were dressed in tree leaves (*SKD.* V. 37). Triśaṅku, after becoming a *caṇḍāla*, was dressed in blue, and so was Mātaṅga (*Kādam.* Kathāmukham of Pūrvabhāga) who wore iron ornaments. According to Manu, *caṇḍālas* used iron ornaments (*MS.* X. 52) and black iron was associated with them (*Vaikh. SM. Sūt.* X. 14).

The *kirātas* and *śvapacas* were hunters; the latter were also fowlers (McCrindle 1973: 52, 85, 88). The former hunted with eagles, ravens, crows and vultures, not with dogs, (*ibid.*) which may mean that the latter hunted with dogs. The Greek sources described the *kirātas* as excellent archers, 3,000 of whom were in the retinue of a king (*ibid.*), probably as bodyguards or soldiers. It is further stated that the *śvapacas* paid tributes to the kings in kind, constructed rafts and traded, along with the *kirātas*, with the neighbouring princes. The *śvapacas* traded amber (gum? *ibid.*, 70) and pigment against cloth, bread, flour, etc. and sold to the peoples of plains bows, javelins, shields and swords (*ibid*., 24), weapons apparently needed for hunting and also in warfare. The *śvapacas* domesticated goats and sheep; the *kirātas* were the domesticators of sheep, oxen, asses and mules (*ibid*.). According to Kauṭilya, *svaganins* had cows and dogs as pets, and the milk of cows belonging to them was for their dogs alone and not for Brāhmaṇas. (*AS*. I. 14). From the Greek accounts also we learn that dogs belonging to the *sunamukhas* drank only cows' milk which made them enormously big and ferocious (McCrindle 1973: 37). According to Manu, the *śvapacas* had both dogs and donkeys; and a *mātaṅga* dogs only. (*MS*. X. 51; *Kādam*. Kathāmukham of Pūrvabhāga).

The *kirātas* brought the rich families from the village, imprisoned them in the forest and took away everything from them. They obtained wives by forcible seizure of others', and stealing wealth from others was their livelihood (*ibid*.). In the *Arthaśāstra*, the *kirātas*, along with hunchbacks and dwarfs, surrounded a king (*AS*. I. 21), here definitely as bodyguards (Chanana 1960: 37). About the *śabaras* and *pulindas*, the former were described as soldiers (*Kādam*. Kathāmukham of Pūrvabhāga), and, according to Kauṭilya, the *śabaras* and *pulindas* probably worked under an *antapāla* (*AS*. II. 1). The *svaganins* roamed in forest to guard against the unlawful entry of enemies and sent signals at their approach. In addition to this, they were to keep watch on *āṭavikas* to stop them from stealing cows, here the *svaganins* working as cowherds (*AS*. II. 29; 34; IV. 5; *Vaikh. Sm. Dh. Sūt*. X. 14-15). The *kirātas* and *mlechhas* were also employed as spies (*AS*. 1.12; IV. 5; XIV. 1).

From the *Arthaśāstra* it seems the *caṇḍālas* were mainly in the employ of a king. A *caṇḍāla* was employed to whip an erring woman in the centre of a village (*AS*. III. 3). He was engaged as a spy to keep watch upon neighbouring kings, should he be trustworthy. The *caṇḍālas* also acted as guards in a fort under an *antapāla* (probably a fort official), and they along with others (*antyavāsayin*) were not to be killed while on duty (*AS*. I. 16). They dragged with ropes the corpses of those committing suicide and threw away the dead bodies outside the village of those having no relatives (*MS*. X. 55; Ruben 1957: 54, 98-99; *AS*. IV. 7). The *caṇḍālas* and *śvapacas* worked as king's executioners as well

(*MS*. X. 56; *Mṛchh*. Ch. 10).

It is not clear whether the *caṇḍālas* were employed in burning all dead bodies. Viśvāmitra found garlands and clothes from dead bodies strewn all over the *caṇḍāla* hamlet (settlement) which indicates their connection with corpses. Triśaṅku also wore a garland from a corpse, and his body was smeared with ashes from funeral pyre. Later evidence points out that the *caṇḍālas* were engaged in cleaning filth from streets and other places (*Vaikh. Sm. Sūt*. X. 14-15).

The *caṇḍālas* were definitely not connected with cleaning latrines, etc. as the sanitary arrangement described in the *Jātakas* and *Arthaśāstra* shows. Latrines and urinals are mentioned separately, not for royal household alone but also for an ordinary blind couple living in a forest (*Jāt*. 540). In the *Arthaśāstra* and also in Aśoka's Rock Edict No. VI, we find mention of latrines (*AS*. III. 8; Bhandarkar 1969: 277. n. 1). In villages it was not necessary to have people for cleaning them as the sites were changed frequently. But, for royal and wealthy families living in towns, it was necessary to have people for cleaning latrines. The work was done by domestic slaves, known as Dāsas (Kane II. 1. 184, n. 430).

The description from the *Mahābhārata* shows not only their settlements as dirty but also their leader as such. But elsewhere *mātaṅga*, at least when he came to visit the king, was dressed in clean and white cloth, and so was the *mātaṅga* girl (*Kādam*. Kathāmukham of Pūrvabhāga). They took meat, alcohol, garlic and onion (*Bṛ. Sūt*. II. 13; Beal 1869: 55; *Kādam*. Kathāmukham of Pūrvabhāga.)

Thus, we find from the foregoing literature that mountains and jungles have been mentioned as dwelling places for some groups of people, who seem to have little or no contact with the village and town people. Either they lived completely separate; or if and when they did have any contact, it was in the nature of causing disturbance and trouble to the inhabitants. To all intents and purposes, they were regarded as outsiders. But an *aryanivāsa* (i.e. where the Aryas lived), as described by Patañjali (*VMB*), consisted of *grāma* (village), *ghoṣa* (pasture land), *nagara* (town) and *samvāha* (caravan route) where the *caṇḍālas* and *mṛtapas* also lived, although the exact spot was not specified. Obviously, the jungles and mountains where the others lived lay in the periphery of particular settlements, which often served as boundaries between two or frontiers of different kingdoms.

The plan of human settlement, as described in the *Jātakas* and the *Arthaśāstra*, supplies some information about the location where different categories of people lived and what their occupations were. From that we may be able to find out who the 'excluded' Śūdras (of Pāṇini) were and where did they live. The following names are mentioned in the *Jātakas* as units of human habitation: *nagara*, *grāma* and *pallī*, *nigama*, *vana/araṇya/aṭavī*, and lastly, *pratyanta grāma* and *pratyanta pradeśa*.

The *nagara* was a town and a seat of royalty, and occupied the innermost place in a settlement. Places like Vārānasi (not Kāśi which was *grāma*), Mithilā and Srāvastī were always mentioned as *nagaras*. The shape of a *nagara* was usually square, but could be rectangular as well (*Age of Imperial Unity*, 484); Mithilā is described in the *Jātakas* as having four main gates on four sides (*Jāt*. 546, 547). The royal families with their staff, soldiers, priests, wealthy merchants and others needing frequent contact with the king lived in a *nagara*. Supposedly they were Kṣatriya, Brāhmaṇa and Vaiśya (*Jāt*. 547).

The *nagara* was surrounded by what is known as *grāma*, the village; the difference between a *grāma* and *pallī* is not very clear from the *Jātakas*. We learn that there were villages designated as those of *kaivarta*, *karmakāra*, *sūtradhāra*, *brāhmaṇa*, *niṣāda* and *caṇḍāla*; and, interestingly, also one of 500 thieves (*Jāt*. 166, 501, 503, 540). As regards a *pallī*, we find that there were *pallīs* of *tantuvaya*, *rajaka* and *caṇḍāla*. Possibly, *pallī* referred to occupation-based streets/areas (*mahallā*?) within a village.

Thus, there are several significant points to be noted about a *grāma*. They are clearly mentioned as being outside a *nagara*. Three types of villages are mentioned. Most of them were occupation based as is evident from such names as *kaivarta*, *sūtradhāra*, etc. (Fick 1920: 181n, 247). Then there were villages of *brāhmaṇa* and *caṇḍāla* (*ibid*.; *Jāt*. 498). Lastly, there were mixed villages where both occupational groups and others lived. For instance, there was a village with a landlord (*bhūsvāmin*) and also a man who cultivated his own land (*Jāt*. 41). In another village there were one thousand families of *śreṣṭhīs* (merchants) and also others (*Jāt*. 546). Another village is mentioned where five hundred thieves lived (*Jāt*. 503).

The size of *grāmas* varied greatly. The largest was where one thousand families lived, the medium-sized had five hundred and the smallest was of only thirty resident families. Thus, villages are mentioned where one thousand families of *kaivarta* or *karmakāra* or *sūtradhāra* lived, and a village of five hundred *niṣādas*. The distance between two villages does not appear to be great as people from neighbouring villages went to a particular village of skilled *karmakāras* to have their iron implements made (*Jāt*. 387).

Another type of settlement, viz. *nigama*, is mentioned. According to Kosambi, this was a tribal settlement in a new territory, in the ancient Roman or Greek sense of colony (Kosambi 1952, Vol. XXVII, Pl. II. p. 186n). It was probably a trading centre too, as traders were reportedly busy in selling their merchandise and also buying from others (*Jāt*. 528).

Next to *grāmas* were probably the forest lands. The following terms for forest are noted: *vana/araṇya/aṭavī*, probably denoting wood, forest and jungle, respectively. The forests do not appear to be very far from the villages and towns, as there were regular contacts of villagers and townsmen with the forests. The carpenters and hunters frequented the forest. A *sūtradhāra* brought wood from the forest (*Jāt*. 492), and a Brāhmaṇa *sūtradhāra* went to a forest along with his workmen to select wood suitable for making chariot wheels (*Jāt*. 475). Some people cleared parts of the forest land for cultivation. Forest products like honey, live birds (caught by *niṣāda*) and venison (the deer caught and killed by a Brāhmaṇa taking up the profession of *niṣāda*) were all sold in a *nagara* (*Jāt*. 533, 543). Apparently, the market was situated in a *nagara*.

Apart from these people frequenting the forests for their livelihood, there were others who roamed or lived in the forest and were known as *vaṇacara* (probably the same as *araṇyacāra* of the *AS*). They hunted animals, sold their meat, and sometimes caught live animals like birds and monkeys, and presented them to the king (*Jāt*. 329). Some of them went from one forest to another, lived there by building temporary sheds, and hunted animals (*Jāt*. 486). In cases of emergency, the forest also provided people with shelter. For instance, king's anger drove one thousand men to the forest (*Jātaka mālā*, 282-83). The subjects of a king fled to the forest with their families, and lived there like animals when life became intolerable because of excessive taxation imposed by despotic king (*Jāt.* 542, 520).

The Jungles were obviously frequented by beasts of prey. The robbers (Dasyus) roamed the forest and harassed the villagers in many ways like extorting money, demanding ransom, stealing merchandise from merchants, etc. There were forest guards whose help was sought and paid for in case of conducting the caravans to safety through jungles (*Jāt.* 513), the amount being as high as one thousand *kārṣapaṇa.* There were also cowpeas in jungles supervised by cowherds (*Jāt.* 349).

Lastly, there were frontier regions and villages (known as *pratyanta pradeśa* and *grāma*). Obviously, the border of a kingdom was marked by its frontier. Frontier regions were not always peaceful, and the subjects often caused trouble to a neighbouring king. Princes were then sent to quell those revolts (*Jāt.* 542). Frontier villages of carpenters and *śreṣṭhīs* are mentioned (*Jāt.* 467), and also mentioned is a large village of *caṇḍāla* near a frontier village (*Jāt.* 474).

While describing a new settlement to be set up by a king, Kauṭilya specified the places where people of each *varṇa*, occupational groups and the *caṇḍālas* should reside. Inside the fort within a settlement (four forts were to be constructed on four sides of a settlement), the northern side was to be the place for deities, Brāhmaṇas and jewellers. On the east resided the Kṣatriyas, perfumers, etc. The southern side was occupied by the Vaiśyas, superintendents for the city, commerce, army, traders, wine merchants, prostitutes and musicians. On the west were the Śūdras and artisans (working on cotton, leather) and those making weapons. The crematoria were to be situated on the eastern and southern sides. People belonging to higher *varṇas* were to be cremated on the southern crematorium, while the eastern one was reserved presumably for the lower *varṇa* people. The *caṇḍālas* lived at the end of the crematoria (*AS.* II. 4).

This exercise in describing the lay-out of a kingdom and/or a settlement by its towns, villages, forests, etc. from the *Jātakas* and the *Arthaśāstra* has been undertaken in order to show the distribution of people, according to their *varṇa* or occupations over the entire region. What can be assumed from the *Jātakas* is that most of the Śūdras, besides those serving in a household, did not live within a town. People not coming in frequent contact with the townsmen appear to have always lived outside (Fick 1920: 280-81, 305-06). Mostly, the occupational groups and also those Brāhmaṇas who followed the occupations of hunters and agriculturists lived out. Possibly, those who needed tools and implements for their jobs requiring large space like the weavers, potters, carpenters, smiths, bricklayers, bamboo workers, dyers, etc. and also those who kept apprentices were located within villages, which were outside a town as they maintained large establishments.

In the *Arthaśāstra* on the other hand, the population was distributed differently. Particular *varṇas* and occupational groups occupied four sides of a settlement. For instance, only north and east were reserved for the Brāhmaṇas and Kṣatriyas respectively. The Śūdras might have lived in the south as well as in the west, while the Vaiśyas could have lived on all the four sides of the settlement. But the *caṇḍālas*, who came under the authority of a king, lived within a settlement but in the vicinity of a crematorium. Significantly, even the corpses were segregated, according to their *varṇas*, as separate crematoria were reserved for higher and lower *varṇas*.

Others, such as, hunters, fowlers, etc. lived outside the village and mostly in forests, according to the *Jātakas*. In the *Arthaśāstra*, too, beyond the settlement (*janapada*) there were mountains, rivers and forests where supposedly others lived. Among them the *āṭavīkas* figured several times. Thus, the argument often advanced that the 'untouchables' were *forced* to live outside a town is not substantiated at least by evidences in the *Jātakas*. There were some people who always lived outside a town or village, as Ambedkar also suggested. However, whether the importance, necessity and nature of their occupations determined their relative distance from the core of a central settlement is not possible to decide yet.

What intrigues one is that, in a region comprising such diverse population, the method of communication among different peoples always posed a problem, as it does even now. During the time of the *Ṛgveda* whether autochthonous people spoke different languages or dialects is not known, but certainly it was not what was spoken by the *RV* people. We find that the Asuras, Paṇis, and *mlechhas* spoke differently from the Aryas (*SPB*, [SBE 26] III. 2.1. 23-24). Vidura was conversant with the language of the *mlechhas* (*Mbh.* I. 135. 6). The *śvapacas*, according to the Greek account, did not speak but only barked (McCrindle 1973: 52, 53). The *RV* people commented on the rustic speech of those they came in contact with, and requested Indra to teach them to use polite words (*Nir.* VI. 31.5). This may imply a completely different language, uncivil speech or pigeon Sanskrit spoken by the local people even after their long association with the *RV* people. The *caṇḍālas* also spoke differently which was unintelligible to those speaking Sanskrit (*Jāt.* 498). Even presently, in Maharashtra, the fifteen subdivisions of *caṇḍālas* speak a peculier language which they do not want to give up under any circumstances (Oppert 1972; 156 n. 50). Obviously, therefore, different forms of speech (or different languages for that matter) existed in society. Nevertheless, we find that *śvapacas* at least could follow the language of the neighbouring people with whom they traded (McCrindle 1973: 53).

Yet what is curious is that the Aryas established a communication channel with the *niṣādas*, as also with the *rathakāras* and *nāpitas*, from the very beginning. Not only that, the *niṣādas* and *rathakāras* observed rituals for which the language was possibly a rudimentary form of Sanskrit. How were they able to communicate with each other? One is tempted to suggest that, even in those days, there were some 'clever' people who quickly learned the language of the 'foreigners' and acted as interpreters until others acquired a working knowledge of it. At least, the parallel case in the recent history of India warrants such a conjecture. As to the ritual language, it is likely that, since the Brāhmaṇas alone officiated the rituals, it was not necessary for the person offering a sacrifice to be well versed in it. Even now, we find that there are many who do not follow the language of a ritual which is performed for them by a Brāhmaṇa. That way the Brāhmaṇas all along held on to their esoteric superiority over others.

However, this gap in the communication continued for quite sometime, narrowing down gradually. The *kirātas* were found acting as bodyguards to a king which could not have been possible without understanding each other. Later, at the time of the epics, to be precise, there appears to be no difficulty for the 'high' to follow the 'low'. That is, both 'King's Sanskrit' and 'cockney' Sanskrit (probably Prākṛt) were freely understood by all. Apparently, Droṇa and Rāma found it not hard to converse with Ekalavya and Guha respectively, although the latter ones were *niṣādas*. Similarly, Rāma communicated with a *śabara* girl, as did Rajavahana (in *Kādambarī*) with Mātaṅga, the son of *pulinda*. A *mātaṅ*ga (i.e. a *caṇḍāla*) girl with her father came to the court of a king where conversation took place between the king and father. Similarly, a *śabara* girl spoke 'cockney dialect', for which she was made fun of. But here there was no difficulty in communicating with those speaking another language (*Kādam*: Kathāmukham of Pūrvabhāga), presumably Sanskrit. Viśvāmitra held a long and serious discourse with a *caṇḍāla* and Kauśika with a hunter who were both definitely in the lowest rung of the social hierarchy, and the conversation was neither casual nor trite. Their discussion ranged from topics like human duty and destiny to religion, philosophy and ethics. Either Sanskrit was their medium of conversation or they spoke regional languages, commonly used by all, which was later 'purified' into Sanskrit for the benefit of all.[3]

Chapter 4

SUMMING UP

WHILE recounting the arrival, advance and settling down of the *RV* Aryas in India, we may designate the first few hundred years or so as an age of military operation, territorial expansion and survival of the *RV* Aryas, when they welcomed the cooperation from the locals. During the initial stage conquest was their main objective, and then survival based on cooperation with the autochthonous groups was on the agenda.

During the second phase, they were busy in consolidating their position and at the same time in arranging the society into different orders with specific duties. While several groups were integrated into their fold, they became powerful enough to express criticism about several others.

The next phase witnessed a situation when the 'untouchables' emerged as an entity. Existing groups were sometime included or excluded from the category of the 'untouchables', and often there was also an extension of its scope. And, lastly, when the *RV* Aryas had entrenched themselves sufficiently in the social organization, the society became rigidly stratified with the 'untouchables' forming a cluster of residual social group.

In this chapter we shall treat these phases separately. The lines demarcating the phases are thin, and there may be interflow within this chronological schema. Chronologically, the first period starting with the expansion and ending in cooperation would have lasted from time immemorial to *ca.* 800 B.C. The literary sources for this particular period are mainly the Vedas, some of the Upaniṣads, Brāhmāṇas Sūtras and the *Nirukta*.

The earliest known phase reveals the Aryas engaged in constant battle with the people in and around the Indus Valley. Obviously, their principal motive was to conquer and subjugate the people occupying the area which they came into. At this stage, therefore, their attitude was 'whoever helps us to achieve this objective is our friend and whoever opposes us is our enemy'. From that perspective the groups of people, mentioned in different types of literature belonging to this period, generally fall under three categories. At one end, there were the Aryas who composed the dominant and the aggressive group—at least the texts give that impression—and their superiority is reflected in the literature. They were the chosen people, the children of god, committed no wrong and whose conduct was beyond question.

Then, in the middle, were the neutral groups in the sense that the Aryas showed none of their enmity or hatred for them. Under this category we find the occupational groups like the barbers, medicinemen, etc. handicraftmen such as *tvaṣṭā/chariot-makers*, ironmongers, metal workers, jewellers, etc. and others engaged in agriculture and animal husbandry. The Aryas, in fact, expressed their appreciation for some of these peoples which is not surprising as they could not do in the beginning without the help of these occupational groups.

At the other end were the hostile groups such as Dāsa/Dasyu, Rākṣasa, Asura, Paṇi, Magadhans, etc. Repeated attempts were made to bring them under subjugation. Of them, we have already hinted at the Dāsas who possibly composed the most powerful group. From the fact that they did not possess grazing ground (or pasture land) we may assume that they were mainly urban people, and were probably not connected with agriculture directly. That the Dāsas were town-dwellers is also indirectly supported by the destruction of a large number of their towns by Indra. Most probably the Dāsas were the people whom the Aryas encountered first during their advance movement through the mainland before penetrating deeper into the countryside. To the Rākṣasas also they maintained the same attitude.

Overt reasons given for the *RV* people's enmity toward these groups were religious, cultural and ethnic. The Asuras did not worship Agni, the god *par excellence* of the Sūras and others were culturally inferior and ethnically different. It was candidly admitted that, since they did not worship the same god or offer sacrifices like the *RV* people, they ought to be subjugated. For the people of Magadha the reason given was that they were non-Aryans, and they were of inferior lineage and of lowly clan.

Noticeably, those whom the Aryas could not conquer were either condemned or harrassed in all possible ways. The Aryas, being unable to control the Asuras, drove them from their hearth and home, and persecuted them in such a way that they were not allowed to stay at one place for long. To the same category belonged Magadha and its people whom the *RV* Aryas found hard to subjugate, while they had their eyes on that region for its wealth. Probably, they were also after a certain type of plant *nīca-śākhā* which grew in abundance there. The Aryas coveted this plant because of its intoxicating juice.

Political and economic factors also influenced the attitude of the Aryas to a great extent. We find the people of Magadha hating the Aryas and supposedly resisting them for quite sometime. The Aryas had strong feelings against the Paṇis as well, who were also traders like the Magadhans and they all lived on usury. To the Aryas, the merchants were niggardly, calculating and selfish by nature. The Magadhans came to be known later as traders mainly, who did not react favourably to the Brāhmaṇical presumptions, for which they were not held in high esteem (Macdonell and Keith 1958: II. 117). But significantly, almost all these groups, with the possible exception of Rākṣasas about whose riches nothing was stated specifically, were wealthy people possessing enviable livestock.

Thus, the *RV* Aryas on their arrival discovered a flourishing civilization based mainly on agriculture. The Aryas, on the other hand, were nomads and pastoral people. But, after coming to terms with the existing local situation, they gave up their nomadic life and settled down. Apparently, it was not a homogenous society, and it was also not a uniform economic system prevailing at that time in north-east India. About the existence of different local groups and of the network of social relationships established by the Aryas there are several direct evidences. But as the economic system we have to rely upon indirect references. The Indus Valley people were a settled agricultural community. They built up their material civilization with wealth derived mainly from grains and cattle. The Aryas, on the other hand, were not familiar with agricultural activities. That they learnt agriculture from the indigenous people is supported by such non-Sanskritic words as *lāṅgala*, *khala*, etc. (Burrow 1955: 379, 382; Thaper 1979: 26), which presuppose the existence of agriculture. This suggests not only borrowing of words but also of learning agriculture by the

Aryas from the locals.

There was another economic sector which seems to have been developed and well organized. Some of the indigenous people were engaged in trading activities, and usury was practised by them. Trading was based mostly on barter system, and cow was the unit of value (Kosambi 1956: 22; Thaper 1966: 36) instead of coins. The Paṇis were traders, and the people of Magadha were both traders and usurers (Macdonell and Keith 1958: I. 158). The *RV* Aryas expressed their hatred for traders, but at the same time they were eager to retrieve cows from the Paṇis and subjugate the people of Magadha. By conquering them and getting their wealth the Aryas wanted to have a control over this area of economy too.

Thus, although enmity with the Magadhans, Asuras, Paṇis, Rakṣasas, etc. was expressed at this stage on ritual ground, it was also strengthened by military failures of the Aryas against them. The purpose of conquest again was motivated by the desire to gain economic control over these people. All these factors were probably expressed through political expediency that was clearly linked up with their attitude to these groups of people.

During the second phase, a significant development took place in the social organization of the Aryas. They now became sure of their position and decided to stay on. Military conquest was no longer the main item on their agenda. Instead, consolidation of their position and the consequent stratification of society on the basis of jobs allotted to categories of people was the policy adopted by them. In all probability, a rudimentary hierarchical division of society was already present among the autochthonous people, but it was now more systematized and well defined because of the contact between the 'outsiders' and 'insiders'. However, this issue of prior existence and later restructuring of social organization is still at the stage of a hypothesis, although buttressed by forceful evidence.

What now emerges concretely is a four-*varṇa* society structured hierarchically by the Brāhmaṇas at the top, next the Rājanya/Kṣatriya, third the Vaiśyas, and the forth and the last the Śūdras. While the duties and jobs of the Brāhmaṇas and Kṣatriyas were specified and limited, those of the Vaiśyas and Śūdras were fluid in nature and were not so clearly defined. Hence the conclusion that all traders, artisans, and workers connected with land and livestock were included under the Vaiśya *varṇa*. The Śūdras were the largest and an amorphous *varṇa*, including all those that did not fit into the other three. Probably, the Dāsa/Dasyu, Rākṣasa, Asura, Paṇi, etc. that is, all those with unspecified occupations, belonged to the Śūdra *varṇa*.

As time passed on, the social sphere of the *RV* people extended territorially and encountered new groups of people. Also, at a place, professional specialization and social division of labour threw a multitude of social groups on the scene. And above all, professional changes revealed the growing sphere of influence of the Aryas. More artisanal and pastoral people, hunters, fowlers, dog-breeders, etc. are mentioned. Simultaneously, we find a fifth category of people (i.e. *pañca*) drawing the attention of the Aryas again and again. This may denote either the number of important families (or peoples) or the settlements the Aryas had brought within their orbit of influence, for the sentiment and attitude of the Aryas toward *pañca* were friendly and conciliatory.

When the Aryas settled down properly, they not only ordered the society into four *varṇas* but actively sought for the cooperation of the local people. The *modus operandi* was either by appeasement or by coercion. The policy of appeasement was manifest in many ways. Status elevation within the social hierarchy was one of them. Many local elites were included in three upper *varṇas*, as pointed out by many reputed scholars. Apart from that, the controversy on *pañca* is a surer indication of it. Of the three main interpretations of *pañca*, two imply the inclusion of influential individuals and/or groups from the aboriginal people.

More clearly, the relationship of the Aryas with the *niṣādas*, *rathakāras* and *nāpitas* was an evidence of this. All of these groups of people whose prior existence is assumed, received favours from the Aryas. Obviously, they were useful to the dominant group in one way or another. The *niṣādas* help was solicited by the Aryas, and they actively helped them to fight the Asuras. Some are of the opinion that *niṣāda* was a generic name for the tribes the Aryas met at this stage, and the *niṣādas* helped them to gain new allies and to penetrate into hitherto inaccessible areas. And the usefulness of a *rathakāra* (i.e. a chariot-maker) to warriors is unquestionable. Only about the *nāpitas* opinions differ, although there is no evidence of their rejection by the Aryas at this stage.

The character of this interaction was later expressed ritually, and this operated at two levels. From among the collaborators, the *niṣādas* and *rathakāras* not only participated in the rituals of the *dvijas* organized by the Brahmaṇas but were also allowed to perform their own rituals independently. The *nāpitas* were an exception to this in the sense that their ritual purity was questioned. Nevertheless, they were allowed to be present at the time of a particular ritual, although not as participants or independent agents. Of all the three, the *niṣādas* were the closest to the Aryas, because they enjoyed the maximum ritual rights; and by the same token the Magadhans were the farthest from them.

At this stage, the social organization of the Aryas was composed of four *varṇas* with job specifications. Obviously, the people at the receiving end of their favours enjoyed high position in the *varṇa* hierarchy. Thus, the *niṣādas* were considered to be Vaiśyas and *rathakāras* the *divijas*. There were also numerous occupational groups of barbers, fishermen, potters, weavers, leather and wood workers, etc. and other unidentified ones like *ugras*, *sūtas*, *kṣattara*, *caṇḍālas* and *śvapacas*; all of them including *mṛtapas* and *dombas* belonged to the Śūdra *varṇa*. Later, the *caṇḍālas* and *śvapacas* were accepted, but the attitude of the Aryas to these groups was not consistent.

Significantly, by this time other groups lost their importance and identity in the sense that they are not mentioned, except the Dāsas. This strengthens the hypothesis that the Dāsas were the most powerful people in the area when the Aryas arrived. By coming to an agreement with them, which is evident from the probable inclusion of their two kings and also from depriving them of the name 'Arya', the *RV* people seemed to have full control over them. The prayer to have one hundred Dāsas, indicating their relatively lower status in society, was a later development. The specific function of a Dāsa, however, is not clear. Were they engaged as domestic servants only or employed in other capacities such as cultivators of their master's field?

Thus, the prayer to possess a large number of Dāsas, the statement that all works (mainly agricultural) do not suit every one and also a mild criticism of weavers tend to show that the Aryas now arrogated themselves to a firm foothold on the extant society. Such an assured position not only indicates their consolidated strength but also that they had probably conquered most of the hitherto hostile groups. From their master-like attitude one may detect the glimmer of the propertied section with need and justification of their comfortable perch. Nonetheless, open condemnation or a clear rejection of any group is not apparent in this period.

The third phase, we may say, starts with the Sūtra literature, that is, from *ca.* 800 B.C. and ends with the *Arthaśāstra* of Kauṭilya which was composed sometime in the third/fourth century B.C. This particular text represents the most reliable and authentic source of information regarding various groups existing in society earlier and also during the time when the author was writing. This phase, that is, the time between *ca.* 800 and 400 B.C. is characterized by the process of integration of various groups into the four *varṇas* in society. The main literary sources for this epoch are the *Nirukta* (of Yāska), *Aṣṭādhyāyī* (of Pāṇini), *Vyākaraṇa-mahā-bhāṣya* (of Patañjali), the Sūtra literature, the Greek accounts and the *Arthaśāstra*.

From all aspects this was an important epoch in India's history. Politically, it was a period of turmoil and turbulence. The powerful Nanda dynasty was overthrown, the Greek invasion took place, the Maurya dynasty was established having Aśoka as its scion, and then its eventual disintegration. The seat of political power was eastern India where, significantly, two important religions, namely, Jainism and Buddhism, also appeared at about the same period. Jainism has a firm foothold in India even today while the other one which became a world religion is disappearing from the country of its brith. Although agriculture was the dominant form of economic activity, this period witnessed also brisk trading activities. Coins were supposedly struck during this time, which was indispensable for large-scale trade and commerce. Increase in population (scholars underscoring it 'population explosion') demanded living space for them. Iron was discovered, and with it clearing of jungles became easier. One finds in the *Arthaśāstra* chapters on clearance of jungles and founding of new settlements. Different dialects were encouraged and enriched through the preachings of Jain and Buddhist monks. All such changes probably helped to break through the isolation of various regions and their peoples, thus bringing them closer than before.

Obviously, all these factors had their impact on the social structure of this period. Some more groups now appear, and specialization is noticed among the earlier ones. Increasing number of forest-dwellers are mentioned by name, such as *kirāta*, *śabara*, *pulinda*, etc. They generally lived in mountains, outlying areas or in the Vindhya forest. Apparently, there were villages inhabited by these people alone. The Jaina monks were warned against visiting a village for alms which was peopled by *mlechhas* (*Ācā. Sūt.* II. 3. 8; 11.17). This may be because they were either hostile to the Jainas or belonged to a different religion, as they were commonly identified with foreigners like the Greeks. People engaged in performing arts (such as dancing, singing and acting) are also mentioned, and artisanal specialization in wood, precious metals, jems and also weaponry took place.

Apparently, not all of them were that close to the core group. As we have seen before, the Śūdra *varṇa* was the end result of the policy of the Aryas while stratifying the society. Since the Śūdras were given the lowest position, one may assume that there was an element of 'coercion' behind this. In any case, while Śūdras were accepted in their social organization, there were others who refused or were refused this 'privilege'. The *RV* people, in the course of their territorial expansion, clearly displaced some and alienated others, which is evident from the etymology of Asura (as explained by Yāska). These people turned into enemies and created disturbance in sacrifice if and whenever possible. There were also the 'excluded' Śūdras whom the later commentators (like Patañjali, etc.) explained as those who were expelled socially, spatially and ritually.

Some of these left-over groups could be brought under control, either by force or by allurement. The *kirātas* found employment with a king as their bodyguards, because they were excellent archers and hunters. The *svaganins* are found to occupy the outermost ring in a cantonment during the war[1], probably because they were expert dog handlers. In all probability, because of their skill with dogs and possibly also because of their riches they were wooed by the authority. The policy of appeasement and/or integration (in the case of the *niṣādas* and probably also of *śabaras*) is noticed in the *Rāmāyaṇa* when Rāma befriended

Guha and went to a hermitage where a *śabara* girl was waiting for her salvation.

But there were still others whom the Aryas (or the centralized political authority) could not bring under complete subjugation. The *śabaras* were not completely under the authority of a king, for they did not know how to serve him. But it was more apparent from Aśoka's edict about the *āṭavikas*, that is, those living in forests. In any case, this period is marked by the attempt to locate the groups within the four-*varṇa* structure of the society, who were otherwise outside the four *varṇas*. For this integration policy some were accepted and some rejected. The *caṇḍālas* were rejected and they lived separately, apparently having no connection with the *varṇa* people. Strangely, though the *mṛtapas* and *dombas* were not spoken of so strongly as the *caṇḍālas*. Sometime the *śvapacas* were also grouped with the *caṇḍālas* and treated similarly. But there was not yet that strong rigidity about them in particular and for others in general.

Here we may cite some mythological and legendary characters, who played such important and strategic roles in the epics, in order to show how that society was not yet so compartmentalized. Probably, these characters belonged to this period or earlier, because notwithstanding their very low origin they were held in high esteem and are considered venerable even today. Vyāsa had a mother who was a fisher-woman and Vidura was born of a Śūdra woman. Both were key figures in the *Mahābhārata*, and, excepting that Vidura was debarred from the throne, they suffered from no handicap or social stigma.

On the contrary, they commanded unqualified respect from all. Parāśara had a *caṇḍāla* (or *śvapaca*) mother, and Vasiṣṭha was born of Urvaśī. On these counts they were never censured in society, Vasiṣṭha is widely known for his religiosity and virtues and even Manu, the ardent champion of *varṇa* purity (among other things), mentioned Akṣamālā who was a *caṇḍāla* (B.C. 49) by way of eulogizing Vasiṣṭha's virtue (*MS.* IX. 23; see also Bühler's footnote). Dīrghatamas begot Kakṣīvat and other *ṛsis* on a maidservant, i.e. a Dāsī (*Bṛhaddevatā* IV. 21.25) who was either a Śūdra or was even lower than that in the *varṇa* hierarchy. Interestingly, according to the Buddhist sources, there were several sages whose mothers belonged to the 'untouchable' castes. For instance, Kaṭha was supposedly born of a foreign woman (*Araṇī*) and Nārada from a maidservant (*tāṇḍulī*); for the latter a reference from the *Bhāgavata* (I. 6. 6-7) is cited (VS. 38). According to the Brāhmaṇical tradition, Viśvāmitra was a Kṣatriya; but a Tāntric text from Central Asia mentions him as *mātaṅgarāja* (i.e. the king of the *mātaṅgas*) and his mother a *caṇḍāla* (*ibid.* 30). Significantly, in the Brāhmaṇical sources also Viśvāmitra's name was associated more than once with the *caṇḍālas*. But, instead of relegating them to the degraded groups of peoples, they were respected in society and accepted in the mainstream of social life. Satyakāma was the 'illegitimate' son of a maidservant. Yet, he was accepted as a pupil by a Brāhmaṇa teacher who appreciated the brave admission of Satyakāma when he revealed his doubly unorthodox origin. Apparently, virtue like truthfulness was valued more than *varṇa* during this period.

The last phase which is partially relevant to the origin of the untouchables falls between *ca.* 400 B.C. and A.D. 1000. The literary sources for this period are mainly the epics, Smṛtis, lexicons, dramas and novels. Politically, this phase was one of unrest, change of dynasties and founding of some of the important empires. The Mauryas were overthrown by the Suṅgas whose rule was short lived, and then followed by the Guptas. The Gupta period was more or less a stable one politically, and the influence of the Guptas spread far and wide.

If the earlier periods were marked by the diminishing hold of Brāhmaṇism on the population because of the tremendous upsurge of Jainism and Buddhism, this period witnessed the triumphant return of Brāhmiṇical orthodoxy in society. Buddhism was virtually driven out of its birth place. Both the Śuṅgas and Guptas were ardent supporters of Hindu doctrines, and the revival of Brāhmaṇism took place with vengeance. Most of the literatures like the epics and the Purāṇas were compiled and rewritten during this period, and there was royal patronage for this task. For Brāhmaṇical theodicy this was really the 'Golden Age'.

Now the power groups directed their attention to reorganizing the social groups. Hitherto the society appears to have had consisted of four *varṇas*, on one side, and, on the other, there were people identified by their respective group affiliation. The main factor of that epoch was that condemnation of certain groups was already in evidence. Now, while the hierarchical division of society was essentially socio-economic, although expressed through religious norms, specialization of occupations and social division of labour proliferated in the society at large. The respective places of all available units were precisely located in the social structure of which the Brāhmaṇas were at the top.

In the course of time numerous units came into existence, some of which were based primarily on their occupations. These occupational units developed gradually into functional castes, and organized themselves into guilds. Merchants' guilds were quite influential, and these were accepted in the mainstream of life and were assigned places in the four *varṇas* (*CHI.* 240, 431; Fick 1920: 258, 267-68; Kosambi 1952: 186).

At this time, the Brāhmaṇas came out with the theory of miscegenation, an attempt to trace the origin of most of the groups in terms of descent from the four *varṇas*. Hence the theory of 'mixed-*varṇas*' (*varṇa-saṁkara*) children, which had started from about the Sūtra period of Sūtra literature (that is, from about *ca.* 800 B.C.), and was followed not only in the sacred literature but also in the grammars, lexicons as well.

In this context, one cannot miss the fact that, in the nomenclature for 'mixed-*varṇa*' children, there was a good deal of agreement regarding the first-order children born of hypergamous unions. It was only when the subsequent orders were discussed (that is, second-, third- or even fourth-order children) that increasing discrepancies were noticed in their names and occupations. Nevertheless, detailed lists of their occupations and names were prepared by many, Manu being one of them. One, however, notices in their names the mention of unidentified groups like the *niṣāda*, *caṇḍāla* etc. occupational groups like *śvapaca*, *kaivarta*, etc. and territorial groups like the *vaidehaka*, *māgadha*. Incidentally, all the earlier groups, except the Magadhans, lost their identity, at least by their names.

In the *varṇa* hierarchy of the Hindus the status of the 'mixed-*varṇa*' children was not always uniform. It was generally accepted, as is natural in a patriarchal society, that *anuloma* sons belonged to the *varṇa* of their father and even Manu accepted such marriages in society. Especially, children born of *anuloma* marriages with the next higher *varṇa* were accepted, as a rule, in the *varṇa* of their father. Therefore, the frequency of *anuloma* marriages and the possibility of children born of such unions were higher than otherwise. The only exception was a *niṣāda*, an alternative name for whom was also *pāraśava* (i.e. a son having a Brāhmaṇa father and Śūdra mother) who was later equated to *caṇḍālas*.

Apparently, both *anuloma* and *pratiloma* marriages started from the highest as well as the lowest *varṇas* in society, as even now breaking of social rules is mostly found in the upper and lower strata of society. That this assumption is not totally unfounded is apparent from the status of some *pratiloma* sons. *Sūta kṣatta* and *māgadha* had all Kṣatriya father or mother. According to majority opinion, an *āyogava* had a Brāhmaṇa mother and a Vaiśya father. But the father of most of the *pratiloma* sons was a Śūdra, and the mother either a Kṣatriya or a Vaiśya. Thus, the *pratiloma* marriages are seen to involve not only the next higher (i.e. the Kṣatriya) and the lower *varṇas*, but, significantly, most of such children were employed in royal household alone (Dattaray 1974). This indicates that their number was not very large, at least to begin with.

But as the number of 'mixed-*varṇa*' children increased in course of time, their absorption in royal households along with specific duties was no longer feasible. Moreover, with the increasing differentiation among the four *varṇas* at all levels any intercourse among them came to be regarded with disfavour. In their elaborate scheme, we find the *niṣādas* and *nāpitas* occupying higher positions as the first-order *anuloma* sons, although the latter was supposed to be born of Brāhmaṇa parents but out of wedlock. The *rathakāras* were downgraded in the hierarchy as it was uncertain whether they should be treated as first- or the second-order *anuloma* sons. But, unlike in the earlier times, the ritual privileges of the *nisādas* and also those of the *rathakāras* were withdrawn.

With the *pratiloma* marriages and their progenies, the situation was complicated and significant. The *pratiloma* children fared worse than those of *anuloma*. Their birth was ascribed to the remiss on the part of a king, and their law of inheritance was different from that of others (*AS*. III. 7). They belonged neither to the *varṇa* of their father nor to that of their mother. The first victims were *caṇḍālas*, *śvapacas* and *sūtas*, involving Brāhmaṇas, Kṣatriyas and Śūdras, mainly in the *pratiloma* order. This shows that the first breach was created in the marriages between the two extreme *varṇas* in society, i.e. the Brāhmaṇas and Śūdras, then with the next higher *varṇa* that is, with the Kṣatriyas.

Of the six possible *pratiloma* sons, even a *caṇḍāla*, supposedly the worst of all, was not hated that much to begin with. But definitely from about the fourth century B.C. (the approximate date of the *Arthaśāstra*), he was ostracized in society, but not the others. *Kṣatta* and *māgadha* belonged to the Kṣatriya *varṇa* and a *vaidehaka* to the Vaiśya *varṇa* (*AK*. 11.8, 59, 97; 111.3, 63), which was quite natural remembering the fact that by profession the *vaidehakas* were traders and that way they should normally belong to the Vaiśya *varṇa*. A *rathakāra* initially had the privilege of a *dvija*, then he became a Vaiśya and later a Śūdra.

Coming to the *Arthaśāstra*, we find that all of them, with the exception of *caṇḍālas*, were ranked as Śūdra, irrespective of the *varṇa* of their parents. Normally, *pratiloma* sons having *dvija* parents could have been treated as *dvijas*. But no. All hypergamous unions not only with the Śūdras but among the *dvijas* also were strongly condemned and the children were the unfortunate victims of their parents' 'folly'. As a result, there was further regrouping and realignment of the different occupational and other unspecified units as it suited the people at the top of societal hierarchy.

In the final phase of their assimilation, we find that the *nābitas*, *mlechhas*, *niṣādas*, *śabaras*, *pulindas* and *kirātas* were not mentioned as the peoples to be 'excluded' from the company of the Aryas. The group that was totally excluded by them was that of the 'mixed-*varṇa*' children. We have already noticed that the six possible *pratiloma* sons were grouped under *antyavāsayin*, and that even by quoting the sage Āṅgirasa the group could not be validated. But what we find significant from their names is that they were neither eponymous nor had any specific jobs like others. On the other hand, some of them had multiple and duplicated jobs, as of the *sūtas* and *māgadhas*.

The earlier suggestion that names for such children were borrowed from existing groups in society is strengthened by the fact that territorial names like the *māgadhas*, *vaidehakas* were adopted for some 'mixed-*varṇa*' children. While making them *antyavāsayin*, one finds it difficult to explain why some groups having not very objectionable occupations were made so, for instance, the *māgadhas*. Is it because they came from a region where Buddhism originated? Or take the case of *vaidehakas*. We find they were traders and harem-attendants. From the *Ṛgvedic* times traders were held in contempt, and it is suggested that, since they were harem-attendants, they were rather looked down upon (Lassen 1847: I. 819). For the *āyogavas* we have already suggested that they probably belonged to matriarchal tribes earlier. It is also suggested that they were probably iron-workers and derived their name from *ayas*, that is, iron. But the problem remains with *kṣattas* and *sūtas*. Previously they enjoyed higher status in society. For some unknown reason(s) they lost that position, and came to occupy a lower one.

We are left with the *caṇḍālas* and *śvapacas* while on the subject of 'exclusion'. Patañjali mentioned two groups, namely, *caṇḍālas* and *mṛtapas* (*VMB*. I. 541), and it seems they were two distinctive and mutually exclusive groups. The *mṛtapas* or *dombas*, as they are frequently referred to, are easier to identify. They lived near a crematorium, collected clothes of corpses, and woods for burning dead bodies (*ibid.*), which shows that they were connected with cremation of dead bodies. A similar group was present in the *Jātakas* in the name of *śavadāhakas*, i.e. those who burn dead bodies (*ibid.*; Jat. 536).

But who were then the *caṇḍālas*? The general consensus is that the *caṇḍālas* were the same whom Ptolemy described as a tribe known as *kandaloi*. In this context, one may quote Ambedkar who mentioned 'Broken Men' as belonging to the group of the untouchables (Ambedkar 1969: XIV. 99). He had probably in mind the *kandaloi* of Ptolemy as one of such broken tribes. But the Hindu, rather Brāhminical, tradition differs from this view. To cite only a few authors in this context. According to the most popular theory, as pointed out earlier, a *caṇḍāla* was the *pratiloma* offspring of a Brāhmaṇa mother and a Śūdra father (*AS*. III. 7.42; *MS*. X. 12), which was followed by the Brāhmaṇa legists. He was also supposed to be the son of an unmarried mother (although there was an alternative term for it, i.e. a *kāṇina*), or a son from a *sagotra* girl, or the offspring of an ascetic turned into a householder (Kane 1941. II. 1.81). Another group, *śvapaca*, has also been identified with *caṇḍāla*. Moreover, some of the non-influential

Buddhists, Jainas and other heretics were probably included among the *caṇḍāla* category, for terms like *pāṣaṇḍa*, *mātaṅga*, *kāpālika*, etc. were made synonymous with it.

The fifteen subdivisions of *caṇḍālas* are mentioned, of which *mādiga* (for *domba* in Maharashtra) is one (Oppert 1972: 156n); and sixteen castes in a village are also treated as *caṇḍālas* in the matter of touch, sight and speech (Kane 1953. IV. 115). There is also the suggestion that the present-day Gonds are the descendants of *caṇḍālas* (Oppert 1972: 156 n. 51). Furthermore, it was not by birth alone but by deeds also that one could become a *caṇḍāla* (Hutton 1951: 150). Because of his misdeeds a king was made a *caṇḍāla* by his subjects. Violation of prevailing norms, be that in marriage, religion, commensality, occupation or deeds resulted in making a particular person or group *caṇḍāla*. Because of this, the definition of *caṇḍāla* kept on changing and adding more and more names to it as time went on. Thus, what was a specific ethnic tribe at one time became a general term over the years (Bose 1942. I. 436, 438-39).

As to the functions of *caṇḍālas*, there was a general agreement. They worked as hangmen of kings, carried corpse of those committing suicide or those having no relatives, and as sweepers of village streets. From the *Mahābhārata* we note that *caṇḍālas* were connected with work at the crematorium and collected the clothes of only those whom they hanged or of those who committed suicide or had no relatives (*MS.* X. 56). For *caṇḍālas*, in general, did not cremate all dead bodies (Fick 1920: 320-21), which was the job of the *dombas/mṛtapas/śavadāhakas*. Incidentally, the coffin-makers, grave-diggers, or those who work in graveyards and are engaged in the disposal of corpses are called *saṇḍāla* in Burma, an obvious similarity with *caṇḍāla* (Hutton 1951: 145).

The *Arthaśātra* and *Manusmṛti* evidence indicates that there were clusters of *caṇḍāla* families living outside every village, depending on the nature of jobs they were supposed to perform for the villagers. The information obtained from the *Jātakas*, on the other hand, gives the impression that they had their own settlements like those of other groups, not necessarily attached to particular villages. The *caṇḍālas* were distinguished by their dress, speech and nature. Quick temper, violence (Lassen 1847. I. 820n) and strong physique are the main characteristics of *caṇḍālas*.

Probably, because of their martial nature, the big landlords of Bengal even in recent times employed them as their club men.

When only the *caṇḍālas* were mentioned as the untouchables, we are not sure whether it applied to the specific or the general category. For, even as late as in the ninth century A.D., it was only the *caṇḍālas* whom Medhātithi considered as untouchables. In any case, from very early times, segregation and redeemable untouchability of *caṇḍālas* were implied, one way or the other, by the *Arthaśāstra, Jātakas* and the *Manusmṛti.* For instance, although their segregation was definite in the *Arthaśāstra,* we do not know whether the *caṇḍālas* had to make their entry into a village known beforehand, so that others could avoid touching them, or, when the daughters of the *śreṣṭhīs* and priests were passing, the *caṇḍāla* stood at one side of the road to make room for them. However, they were probably known by their dresses, so that they could be recognized immediately as *caṇḍālas.* But their segregation as well as untouchability became an established fact by the beginning of fifth century A.D. as recorded by Fa-Hien.

At what point of time in history did untouchability appear in society? Here, we have to bear in mind that no phenomenon emerges suddenly in society. It is always a gradual process lasting over a long period. The beginning is often hidden or hazy, and it becomes visible only when the phenomenon assumes a definite form. With untouchability also it is the same. What appeared, maybe from the *Ṛgvedic* and Upaniṣadic times, as rudimentary and insignificant, emerged as a full-fledged institution, gathering strength and gaining proportion over the ages. In this context, several indirect evidences may help us in deciding the time factor in the emergence of untouchability.

Although the word *caṇḍāla* occurred earlier, their untouchability was mentioned later. For instance, if the indicators for untouchability are accepted as those of physical segregation (from the caste groups), not to be seen and touched (again by the same groups), non-commensality and non-connubiality following from the above factors, and, lastly the specific Sanskrit word for untouchables (*aspṛśya*), the source materials belonging to the period between *ca.* 400 B.C. and A.D. 200-400 testify to one or the other factor. For instance, the factor of segregation has been noted in the *Arthaśāstra*, the *Jātakas*, and probably in the accounts of Fa-Hien. The taboo regarding sight and touch is described clearly in the *Jātakas*. Ptolemy, who mentioned *kandaloi* as a tribe and which was later identified with *caṇḍāla*, belonged to the second century A.D. (Vigasin 1985: 21).

The vertical division of Śūdras and the dichotomy between *sat* (pure) and *asat* (impure) Śūdra resulting in making some of the latter 'untouchable' started from about the Gupta period (Sharma 1980: 323). And above all, the word *aspṛśya* (untouchable) with its present connotation occurred in *Viṣṇusmṛti*, *Gant. Dh. Sūt.*, Fa-Hien, etc. all belonging to this period.

Significantly, the above phase showing a marked development/change in the status of the untouchables is also characterized by basic social and economic changes taking place in the history of India. This is demonstrated by two important Sanskrit texts, the *Arthaśāstra* of Kauṭilya and the *Manusmṛti*. The former is a treatise on political economy and the latter is the 'Hindu Code'. Both the texts describe society in its various aspects and also the changes recommended by the authors. The *Arthaśāstra* depicts a society with autarchy. The king was supposed to have direct and strict control over all forms of production, which suggests maintaining a huge bureaucracy by the state. Thus, we find that products from agriculture, forestry, animal husbandry, lakes and tanks, etc. were directly supervised and collected by the king's officials in the crown colony. As regards agriculture, which was the dominant form of production, the ownership of land in the crown colony was conditional. If the land was developed by the state, the ownership was given to a person for one generation only. In the case where the land was developed on private initiative, the person was allowed to retain his ownership (*AS*. II. I). This probably applied both to the lands in the crown colony as well as to those of the private owners. For agriculture and other forms of production were carried out simultaneously in the crown colony and in places beyond it but within the political jurisdiction of a king.

The king was also in charge, through officials, of managing, supervising, leasing out and collecting taxes from trade and commerce, mining and manufacturing industries (*AS*. II. 12). Details like employment of labour or specified jobs and payment of their wages, collection of taxes, etc. were mentioned and also of punishment for their violation at every stage. Market towns were set up where merchandise, produced within the crown colony and also coming from country parts, were sold to buyers (*AS*. II. 16).

There were usually three main sources of revenue to the treasury. From agriculture the usual tax was one-sixth of the produce, the size of the holding remaining unspecified. There was, in addition, irrigation tax, the amount varying on the methods by which water was carried to the field (*AS*. II. 24). Tax-free lands were also granted to some types of Brāhmaṇas (*AS*. II. 1) and to some officials (in lieu of salary?) without the right of alienation in the latter case (*ibid.*). Villages supplying soldiers, grains, cattle, gold, raw materials and free labour were exempt from taxes (*AS*. II. 35; III. 10). The second major revenue-yielding source was trade and commerce, where almost at every stage, right from the production to the selling places, different types and rates of taxes were to be paid by the trader and merchant (*AS*. II. 21, 22, 25). The last were the emergency cases and special heads when and under which taxes were levied on the people (*AS*. II. 15), the amount probably not always small. We have noted from the *Jātakas* how excessive taxation drove the subjects of a particular king to the forest.

Administratively, villages were grouped into units of 10, 200, 400 and 800 (*AS*. II. I). A *grāmika* was a village headman, then there were persons in charge of cities and a *sthānika* probably looked after a town. A *gopa* (village accountant) maintained detailed registers of the inhabitants under his jurisdiction, which could be either five or ten villages, and he was also in charge of ten, twenty or forty households. The *gopas* and *sthānikas* were under a *pradeṣṭṛ* who looked after the works and the means employed, and also collected *bali*. A *samāhatṛ* was specially employed for the capital city (*AS*. II. 35.).

Free labour was extracted, the period or frequency not mentioned, from the following persons: sweeper, preserver (guard?), persons weighing or measuring grains, supervising the supply of commodities to the store house, receiver of complaints in connection with grains, slaves and workers (*AS*. II. 15). Except the last one who was probably a free worker, all others seemed to have been employed by the king.

Attempts at such total and strict control through state machinery is also reflected in the social sphere which was not yet uniform. Two types of marriage indicated two segments of society, one offering more choices to women and the other restricting the scope of them. Gradually, however, the role of family property, its inheritance and the performance of *śrāddha* by an innate son became a dominant feature of society, underlining thereby the growing importance of the latter segment (Mukherjee 1978) which was obviously also the propertied section.

Further, we note that during this phase the dominant social units in society were no longer the *varṇas*. Instead, the *jātis* (i.c. the birth of an individual in a particular group which may be called caste) emerged which is hereditary and immutable.

It appears that *varṇa* division was no longer suitable, and, therefore, further division was created. One can argue that the section offering less alternatives to women in the interests of perpetuating the lineage and property consisted of higher *varṇas*, that is, presumably the Brāhmaṇas and Kṣatriyas. Logically, therefore, these people would want to maintain their 'exclusiveness' in so far as their economic and social privileges were concerned. Apparently, a *varṇa* was too large and less well defined an institution for this purpose. A smaller and better-knit social organization was required now. Consequently, further and finer stratification was felt necessary when more and more new groups had to be accommodated (and/or assimilated, and also who came into existence) because of expanding economy and job specialization. Hence a small unit like *jāti* which expressed detailed ranking by locating each new entrant was more suitable for the present need.

Even if the *varṇa* system was elastic, the *jāti* division was static. Moreover, while *varṇa* permitted exogamy and certain amount of mobility, *jāti* division allowed only endogamy and perpetuated the hereditarily determined occupation pattern in society. The hereditary aspect of *jāti* was strengthened at the ideological level by the doctrine of *karma* and transmigration of soul (Mukherjee 1957).

Such all-encompassing economic activities as suggested by Kauṭilya obviously affected the entire population within a particular area. Gradually, individual and group producers (in the form of guilds) lost their independent role in the process of production. Clearance of jungles and bringing under control the waste and forest lands disturbed the people living there (Kosambi 1956: 228). Most of them were probably hunters and food-gatherers, living on the yields of the forest and selling the surplus produce either to the king or in the market. They continued to lead their life until the political aggrandizement of a particular king and the market condition, on the one hand, and the depletion of the natural resources (of the forest), on the other, disrupted their life and forced them out of their isolation. With the spread of agricultural economy the scope of arboreal economy was thus gradually narrowed down. Some of the displaced persons did find employment with the king, and others were left to work probably as free labourers.

The *Manusmṛti*, on the other hand, was not concerned so much with these details as it was primarily a Brāhmaṇical code where ethical and religious topics (from the Brāhmaṇical point of view) were mainly discussed. The picture that emerges from it is that of a stabilized society, both economically and socially. The king appears less despotic and his control less rigid. His area seems a little larger in the sense that the maximum number of villages mentioned was one thousand (*MS*. VII. 114-15). The administration appears more flexible and responsibilities delegated. The smallest administrative unit consisted of two, three or five villages (*ibid*), each village having a headman, and then 10, 20, 100 and 1,000 villages having different heads respectively (*ibid*). A *sarvārthacintaka* was appointed for each city—*nagara* (*MS*. VII. 121). Instead of wages, the headmen were probably granted the right to own cultivable lands and/or enjoy revenue from villages. Thus, a headman of ten villages enjoyed one *kūla*, that of two villages five *kūlas*, that of 100 villages one village and that of 1,000 villages one town—*pura* (*MS*. VII. 119; Bühler's footnote also).

A *grāmika* collected from the villagers what was to be given to the king, that is, food, drink and fuel (*MS*. VII. 118). It is not clear whether these were appropriated by the *grāmika* or were sent to the king. Tax was collected annually by the king, and the persons, period and frequency of free labour were clearly specified. Mechanics, artisans and those Śūdras living on their own labour should each render free labour to the king one day every month (*MS*. VII. 138). The usual tax from the cultivators seems to have been one-sixth but could also be one-eighth or one-twelfth (*MS*. VII. 130); in time of emergency it could have been one-fourth while from the Vaiśyas it was one-eighth of paddy (*MS*. X. 118, 120).

This stable picture of the economic order is also reflected on the social aspects of life. It appears as if the transitional phase of the society as depicted in the *Arthaśāstra* and which was also the emergent trend had been fully consolidated. The Brāhmaṇical orthodoxy prevailed in all spheres of life, and so was it in the case of *caṇḍālas*. In the *Arthaśāstra*, they were treated as a segregated, ritually impure group but possibly not yet as untouchables. For an adulterous woman was not made an outcaste, although she was whipped by a *caṇḍāla*. Moreover, some of them, according to Kauṭilya, could have been employed by a king. But in the *Manusmṛti*, their segregation, degradation, ritual as well as social inpurity, became the established order. The *caṇḍālas* became total rejects in society.

Reason(s) behind the derogatory attitude toward the *caṇḍālas* is hard to explain. It is often argued that 'purity and pollution' was the cause of making them the most despised group and untouchable in society. Fick and Ambedkar had already questioned the validity of the theory of 'purity-pollution' and considered it as a later imposition (Fick 1920: 325; Ambedkar 1969: xiv). Nevertheless, it was claimed by many social scientists as the cause of untouchability. The confusion was probably created by the fact that, whatever the real reason(s) of the origin of untouchability was, it was blurred by a long period of time (see also Ambedkar 1969: xvii). And religion successfully tied up the loose ends and rounded its sharp edges. Consequently, trees are missed for the woods, and 'purity-pollution' appears as the cause of untouchability. However, the smoke-screen was cleared up by Lynch and Sharma who adroitly argue that it was the effect and not the cause of untouchability. As a counter-arguement, it can be pointed out that there were other groups of people who performed cruel (like hunters), impure (like *mṛtapa*, *dombs* or *śabadāhaka*) or dirty (like those Dāsas cleaning latrines) jobs. Nowhere a *caṇḍāla* was specifically referred to in connection with any of these jobs, except indirectly to hunting (by the *niṣādas*) and directly to dealing with some types of corpses. Thus, if 'purity and pollution' were the main criteria for making the *caṇḍālas* the worst group then there were others who performed worse jobs in society. But no such antipathy was shown to them. Apparently, the notion of 'purity-pollution' was the secondary attribute applied to the *caṇḍālas* alone.

Similarly, religion was not the main factor behind making some people untouchable, because all those who collaborated with the Aryas did not belong to the same religion or practised the same rituals. For instance, the *niṣādas* were sun worshippers whereas the Aryas worshipped Agni. But this religious difference did not impede the Aryas in cooperating with the *niṣādas* especially when the latter helped the former actively. That collaboration preceded religion becomes more evident in the case of Kikata and its people. Like the *niṣādas* they also belonged to another faith. But, as they did not cooperate with the Aryas, religion in their case gained undue importance. Nevertheless, they were not mentioned as untouchables probably because of their significant socio-economic position in society.

The problem, therefore, remains why the *caṇḍālas* alone were made untouchables and not others. One cannot fail to note that, whenever anything was mentioned about them, the prevailing attitude toward the *caṇḍālas* was tinged, as if, with a spirit of 'vengence', although there is no evidence of any direct confrontation with this group in particular. Only the *śabaras*, as we already know, never served a king, which indicated their non-allegiance to a centralized political authority. About others, who were often synonymous with or included under the category of *caṇḍālas*, no such specific information is available.

There was another group, the *āṭavikas*, who were singled out for censure. But unlike the *caṇḍālas*, there is evidence of confrontation with the *āṭavikas*. The *Arthaśāstra* furnishes some details about the relationship of the *āṭavikas* with the existing political authority. They often created trouble to a king who also did not trust them. The tension between the king and the *āṭavikas*, or maybe between him and all forest-dwellers for that matter, and the disobedience of the latter, was of long standing. From the *Jātakas* also we find that people of the frontier regions occupying forests caused disturbances, and revolt broke out from time to time (see also Fick 1920: 106). Then there were the *āṭavikas* whom even Aśoka found hard to bring under control. They must have been 'difficult' and 'troublesome' enough to evoke such a stern posture from him in spite of his contrition. This threat to 'kill' coming from a repentent king shows that the *āṭavikas* posed a serious danger to a king. They were supposed to be wild tribes not yet Aryanized (Kosambi XXVII. Pt. II. 205). Even during the Gupta period there were as many as eighteen such tiny forest kingdoms known as *aṭavī rājya* (Bhandarkar 1969: 42) whose people were not subordinate. They were independent or quasi-independent, sturdy, proud and freedom-loving ethnic groups of people.

But who were the *āṭavikas*? Did the term include others or was it a distinct group, separate from others? Etymologically, it means people living in an *atavī* (i.e. forest). There were also general terms for forest-dwellers such as *araṇyacara*, *vanacara*, etc. as mentioned by Kauṭīlya and in the *Jātakas*. What, however, is not clear whether such general terms as *araṇyacara*, *vanacara*, and *āṭavikas*, all of whom referred clearly to forest-dwellers, were separate from groups like *kirāta*, *śabara*, *pulinda*, etc. Or, they were all included under the blanket term of *araṇyacara* or *āṭavikas*.

The latter hypothesis seems more credible as different groups have already been mentioned living in forests. Therefore, if the *āṭavikas* are taken as a general term embracing all forest-dwellers, the next problem is whether there was any connection between them and the *caṇḍālas*. Although there is no direct evidence to link them up with the *caṇḍālas*, probably as with other forest groups, the *āṭavikas* also later came to be regarded as *caṇḍālas*. At least the people of the *aṭavī* country were found to be mentioned side by side with *pulindas* and others (Bhandarkar 1969: 42), and *pulindas* belonged to the *caṇḍāla* category. There is also evidence to show that, whenever anyone or any group went against the existing norms in society, they were regarded as *caṇḍālas*. For example, it has already been mentioned that apostates and sons of unmarried mothers were all *caṇḍālas*. If Karṇa were born a little later (i.e. later than the *Mahābhārata* period), he would have been considered a *caṇḍāla*. And the *pratiloma* sons—*śvapacas*, *mātaṅgas*—were definitely placed in the *caṇḍāla* category, and the *kirātas* and *śabaras* indefinitely, which strengthens the surmise that *caṇḍāla* was a general term (Bose 1920. I. 438-39).

Caṇḍāla category was as if the last refuse of all unwanted people. This group not only kept on swelling in number but also consisted of diverse elements. Possibly, therefore, the *āṭavikas* also, like others, merged with the *caṇḍālas* after sometime, and the former lost identity in due course. This is further strengthened by the fact that later most of the other social groups lost their names and identities but not the *caṇḍālas*. This is supported not only by the structural composition of the *caṇḍālas* but also by the fact that unlike other eponymous caste groups like *rajakas carmakāras*, etc. *caṇḍālas* indicate neither any specific occupation nor any definite occupation was prescribed for them.

Significantly, this method of mixing diverse peoples under a common label and then giving them the lowest position in society is not new. Indian social system, in spite of its rigid structure, developed organizational 'devices' for absorbing unwanted and 'alienated' groups of people, which also acted as 'safety valves'. Through such measures not only all the 'misfits' had a place within the social scheme of the Hindus but they also achieved the desired distance to be maintained between the beneficiary and non-beneficiary groups. From the time of the *Ṛgveda* one notices that some groups were accepted and others rejected by the core as the situation demanded. This not only changed the alignment of social forces frequently, but one also notices in this process the gradually increasing control by some groups and the downward movement of others.

For instance, initially, the *dvijas* occupied the central position, and the Śūdra *varṇa* was the lowest and the 'safety valve' accommodating the non-Aryas, Dāsa/Dasyu and other conquered peoples. Whoever could not be included under the three upper *varṇas* came to be known as Śūdra (Bhandarkar 1940: 5). Still the Śūdras were considered a part and one of the four *varṇas*.

Then the anomalous *pañcama* appeared with its varying interpretations. Whenever the *varṇa* or caste identity of a group was open to doubt, it was included under *pañcama* (Macdonell and Keith I. 466-68). Sometimes the *niṣādas* (including the 'mixed-*varṇa*' children), or the *caṇḍālas*, or the Jainas were considered *pañcama* (Sangave 1959: 105). Probably, there was a controversy whether *pañcama* should be regarded as a *varṇa*, because Manu declared that there could never be a fifth *varṇa*. Thus, by its nomenclature, *pañcama* was the fifth category but not a *varṇa* and this time those at the top of the hierarchy were powerful enough to keep it separate from the four-*varṇa* society.

Now comes the turn of the *caṇḍālas*. To begin with, it was a specific one like any other group as identified by Ptolemy and also as mentioned in the texts. But later it became a generic term embracing many other social groups and individuals which is supported by its ever-changing and ever-expanding scope. It seems as if the orthodox Hindus were faced with the problem of defining or identifying this uncertain group. Therefore, all the 'dregs' of the Hindu society were grouped together under *caṇḍāla*. But this time they were neither one of the four *varṇas* like the Śūdras, nor were they the doubtful *pañcama*. They were definitely cast aside by the Hindus, and were a condemned group outside the Hindu society.

Now the problem is why the designation of *caṇḍāla* was selected and why did all others agree to merge with them, accept a new identity by giving up their own? Presumably, the *caṇḍālas* formed an influential group, probably powerful too, among all the forest-dwellers. The following factors point to their distinctiveness as well as to their separate status from others. The word *caṇḍāla* was originally not a Sanskrit (Lassen 1847: I. 820 n; Sharma 1980: 336) but an un-Aryan word (Mayrhoffer 1956. I: 370), which implies its antiquity. They had their own identity in the sense that they had their language, the *caṇḍāla-bhāṣā* (*Jāt*. 498). Only two other groups, that is, the *mlechhas* and Asuras has their own languages. But they, according to definitions, were not specific groups like the *caṇḍālas*. There was also a particular root vegetable which owed its name to the *caṇḍālas*, the *caṇḍāla-kanda*. (Monier-Williams 1951: 383). This indicates not only their long association with forest products but also their importance which made the vegetable to be named after them. The *caṇḍālas* must have been a care-free people. They played a lute which came to be known after them, the *caṇḍāla-ballaki* (*Jāt*. 531, 498; Monier-Williams 1951; 383; Oppert 1972: 32), and only they knew the art of blowing a particular type of flute (*caṇḍāla-vaṁśa-dhopana*

(Fick 1920: 318; see also Bose 1942: 439-40).

Therefore, one can assume that other groups acknowledged the superiority of the *caṇḍālas* (for whatever reason it might be), although one wonders why *sūtas*, who were respectable and influential enough, were deprived of that honour. Admittedly, all the groups living in forests and mountains did not have the same degree of social development. From the Greek as well as Brāhmaṇical sources we find evidence of unequal development among different groups. The *śvapacas* were the most advanced in the sense that their society was stratified, that they possessed technical skill and maintained trade relations with neighbouring kings. The least developed were the *śabaras* who seemed to be backward, wore tree leaves and did not have any relation with the established political power. Other groups like *pulindas*, *kirātas*, etc. were not that important, except that the latter were good archers. It may not be unlikely that, when the questions of marger came up, other groups were weak to offer any opposition. The only strong group was that of the *śvapacas* who could offer a viable opposition. They could have insisted on their name to be retained. Here, probably, political power intervened by defeating them, and the Brāhmaṇa legists retaliated by making them even lower genealogically, than the *caṇḍālas*. As if to assuage them, they were equated to *caṇḍālas*. Supposedly, *caṇḍāla* as a name was more important to be retained and continued.

It is still not very clear why the *caṇḍālas* had been hated so much in society. To ascribe this merely to ritual and social transgressions may not be adequate. The circumstantial evidence, in the absence of any other, may be of help in finding an answer. What is significant in this context is that from the beginning there is neither any evidence of cooperation nor of non-cooperation of *caṇḍālas* with the Aryas. We have noted earlier that whoever cooperated with the Aryas initially were accepted within their fold. But the *āṭavikas* definitely and the *caṇḍālas* probably did not.

Probably, the situation would have been different if they were left to themselves. But they could not live in isolation for long. To the growing political and economic influence of the ruling group they had to surrender. With the scope of arboreal economy becoming restricted and encroachment on their land taking place, the *caṇḍālas* (and others too) had to come out of the seclusion, a parallel case noted recently about the Sāntāls. Deprived of their habitat and livelihood, some of them accepted the 'munificence' of their 'masters'; but others did not. Even very recent history shows the *caṇḍālas* as a proud group of people, who zealously guarded and maintained their separate identity and freedom as long as possible.

And, probably, it was not easy to bring them under control. It was the 'rebels' who suffered most, because the erstwhile enmity with and insubordination of the *āṭavikas* in particular and of *caṇḍālas* in general was neither forgotten nor forgiven. When they were brought under subjugation eventually, they were neither incorporated into the main economic activity prevailing at that time, that is, agriculture, nor into any other form of production in society. Only unskilled, unproductive, lowly and menial jobs were assigned to them. Thus, when they were forced to surrender it was not clemency they received. Instead, they were treated with utter contempt and were segregated as a residual category of people to be employed as and when necessary.

Notes

Introduction

1. Surveys on castes and tribes in different parts of India were first initiated by the British probably in 1869 (*Memoire of the Races of the North Western Provinces of India*, 2 Vols., Sir H.M. Elliot). From 1891 (Risley, *Tribes and Castes of Bengal*) systematic data on castes and tribes were collected for helping the British in administering India. These were mainly ethnographical studies which even today serve as bed-rock for researches on castes and tribes in India.

2. The two terms, *varṇa* and *jāti* are often confused probably because of the blanket term 'caste' which is indiscriminately used both for *varṇa* as well as for *jāti*. In order to avoid this confusion, I have refrained from using the word 'caste', unless absolutely necessary. If at all, 'caste' will be used only in the sense of *jāti*. (In this context, see Mukherjee, 1957: 62-66).

3. At the time when it was used by Gandhi in the early thirties, although the term was first suggested by a poet-saint of Gujarat (Gupta 1985: 30), it appeared that he gave an honourable name to the untouchables by calling them 'Harijan'. It was even sincerely believed that at last here is the identity which they have been searching for. But now very few make use of this term. 'They feel it connoted the idea of being a bastard and also brought to mind patronising upper caste benevolence' (Lynch 1969: 31).

4. After World War II, however, the field is increasingly crowded by American anthropologists and sociologists. Untouchability in India is probably somewhat parallel to the Black problem in the USA. To quote Lynch: 'Untouchability in India, like discrimination in the United States, has become a pejorative term; one must avoid publicly practising either' (*ibid.*, p. 210).

5. It was a happy coincidence to find the same opinions expressed by Lynch and Sharma. 'Socially constituted differences among men are the source and origin of the fundamental belief underlying purity and pollution' (Lynch 1978: 120; see also Mukherjee 1982: 187-90 on Sharma 1980: 146, n. 4).

6. That only urban settlement requires the services of such people is not disputed. But who cleaned the soak-pits, drains, etc. in Mohanjodaro and Harappa? Since that time to that of the *Arthaśāstra*, we do not find any evidence of them. That Kauṭilya forbids a pledged slave to touch dead bodies, remove human excreta, etc. shows that there were others doing such jobs. Who were they? (See also Ambedkar 1969: 84; *AS.* III. 13).

Chapter 1: Enumeration, Condemnation and Cooperation

1. From later evidene, however, the Aryas came to be synonymous with Vaiśyas (*AV.* XIX. 32. 8; *AK.* II. 9. 1; Lassen 1847. I. 795), and no longer the self-styled people of the *RV* as mentioned earlier.

2. Sharma differentiates between the Dāsas and Dasyus, the former being mentioned sixty-one times and the latter eighty-four times in the *Ṛgveda.* While the *Ṛgvedic* Aryas were openly hostile to the Dasyus, toward the Dāsas their attitude was less so. He argues that the Dāsas were possibly 'an advance guard of mixed Indo-Aryan peoples who came to India' and in the course of time the Dāsa came to be bracketed with all other pre-Aryan peoples like the Dasyus, Rākṣasas, etc. (See Sharma 1980: 11, 16-17, 25-27, etc.). Other sources, however, seem to make no difference between the Dāsas and Dasyus (Macdonell 1963: 157). They were equated to Iranian Daha and Dahyu and considered to be Dravidians (Chatterji 1974: 9).

3. In *Nighaṇṭu* I. 1.2, fifteen names are mentioned which are synonymous with *hiraṇya,* among which *ayas, loham* are found. Either *hiraṇya* was not gold but a generic term for all metals, or gold being the earliest known metal, others were equated to it (*RV.* VIII. 77. 11).

4. Kosambi observes that 'tools of violence were curiously weak ... among the Indus valley finds' (Kosambi 1956: 59). Inequality in society was maintained not with weapons but with religion perhaps (*ibid.*).

5. Following Ptolemy, Sharma equates the śūdra to *sydroi.* But while Muir thinks it was an indigenous tribe (Bhandarkar 1940: 5), according to Sharma they also come to India, like the Dāsas (see Sharma 1980: 34-36, 39-40). It seems the Śūdra *varṇa* included anyone other than an Aryan, even a foreigner (Bhandarkar 1940: 5) and gradually 'large numbers of aborigines of varying stocks were successively incorporated in the śūdra *varṇa,* (Sharma 1980: 33). Thus, even if their identification is an open question (i.e. whether or not they were indigenous people), the borrowing of their name is a distinct possibility, as suggested later in the parallel cases of *anuloma* and *pratiloma* children.

6. Interestingly, Pracinasala, with the patronymic of Aupamanyava, i.e. son of Upamanyu, was one of the five enquiring after Eternal Truth from the king of Kekaya (*Chh. Up.* chaps. 11 and 12 of Book V).

7. See Mukherjee 1981: 19-26.

8. Significantly, there is a Jaina caste in the Deccan known as *pañchama.* While tracing their origin, they assert that the Vedic Brāhmaṇas during the ninth and fifteenth centuries A.D. considered the Digambara Jainas as outside four *varṇas.* Consequently, the Jainas called themselves as *pañchama* (Sangave 1959: 105).

Chapter 2: Indentification, Rejection and Segregation

1. Indian dogs were prized so much that people of four Babylonian villages breeding Indian dogs for hunting and war were exempted from paying

taxes by the Persian Emperor Artaxerexes I (465-424 B.C.) (Stutley 1977: p. 294, n. 3).

2. The word *apapātra* (lit. when a vessel used by one of lower *varṇa* cannot to used by higher *varṇa* people) had been used in relation to *caṇḍālas* and others like *pratilomas*, washermen, etc. (*Āpas. Dh. Sūt*. I. 7. 6, 17; II. 7. 17. 20; *Baud. Dh. Sūt*. I. 11. 17; *MS*. X. 51). It gained currency when non-commensality with *caṇḍālas* was advocated. It was suggested that food to the *caṇḍālas* (and others like them) should be served by the upper caste people on a broken plate, or the plate used by them should be thrown away; for such a plate (or vessel) could never be 'pure' even after it was cleaned (Kaś. Vāmana 1931: 92; Vasu I. 312).

3. Even Kauṭilya condemned the *pratiloma* marriages and children born of such unions (*AS*. III. 7).

4. It seems only male children were segregated and not the female ones. But female *pratiloma* children were victimized in respect of their marriages.

5. This is discussed in greater details in my paper 'Toward Identification of Untouchable Groups in Ancient India, as enumerated in Sanskrit Lexicons' *The Journal of the Asiatic Society*, Vol. XVI. 1974, pp. 1–14, Calcutta.

6. The mention of *antevāsin* is rather strange as it is generally used for co-disciples.

7. And even that could not be located yet, for, in the extant Smṛti and Saṁhitā ascribed to Āṅgiras, the *śloka* on *antyavāsayin* is not mentioned. Later digest writers like Viśvarūpa, Haradatta (Kane 1930. I. 221, 222), Raghunandan, however, mentioned the above *śloka* as having been propounded by Āṅgiras. From several quotations mentioned by Raghunandana in his *Aṣṭaviṁśatitattvam*, it appears that he had been quoting from the extant *Āṅgiraḥsmṛti* (see under *Smṛitināmsamuccaya*), which, however, does not contain the *śloka* on *antyāvasāyin*. On the other hand, although not mentioned in any of the lexicons, the *śloka* on *antyaja* is found there (*Āṅgiraḥsmṛti* 3).

Chapter 3: Life and Living of the Untouchables

1. Is it an attempt to counteract the Jaina and Buddhist influence in society?

2. In the *RV*. IV. 18. 13, too, there is a reference to cooking dogs' entrails by Vāmadeva obviously for the purpose of eating.

3. Parenthetically once, while discussing the problem of language with my teacher, Professor Walter Ruben, he told me that the major or probably the only contribution of the Indo-Aryans was their language, i.e. Sanskrit.

Chapter 4: Summing Up

1. According to Herodotus (VII. 187), the army of Xerexes was followed by a large number of Indian dogs while invading Greece (Stutley 1977: p. 294, n. 3).

REFERENCES

A. Texts

Ācaraṅga and *Kalpa-sūtra*. SBE. Vol. 22 Pt. I. H. Jacobi (ed.).

Amarakośa. 1929. Pandit Vishnu Dutta Sharma (ed.). Bombay.

Āpastambiya-dharma-sūtra. 1932. Sanskrit Series, Nos. XLIV and L. 3rd edn. George Bühler (ed.). Bombay.

The Arthaśāstra of Kauṭilya. 1925. 3 Vols. T. Ganapati Sastri (ed.). Trivandrum.

Aṣṭādhyāyīsūtrapāthaḥ. 1954. Bombay: Nirnayasagara Press.

Aṣṭaviṁśatitattvaṁ (of Raghunandana). 1347 (Bengali era). Shyamakanta Vidyabhusan (ed.). Calcutta.

Aśvaghoṣer Buddha-carita. 1352 (Śāka era). 2 Vols. Rathindranath Tagore (tr.). Visva-Bharati.

Āśvalāyanagṛhyasūtram. Ānandāśrama Saṁskrita Series, No. 105.

Atharva-veda-saṁhitā. 1971. 2 Vols. W.D. Whitney (tr.). Delhi: Motilal Banarsidass.

Atrisaṁhitā. See *Smṛtinām Samuchchaya*.

The Baudhāyana-gṛhya-sūtra. 1904. L. Srinivasacharya (ed.). Bibliotheca Sanskrita, No. 32. Mysore.

Baudhāyana-dharma-sūtra. 1934. Kāśi Sanskrit Series, No. 104. Benaras.

Bṛhad-āraṇyaka Upaniṣad. 1965. 4 Vols. Durgacharan Sāṁkhya-Vedānta-tīrtha (ed. & tr.). Calcutta.

Bṛhaddevātā of Sauṇaka. 1965. A.A. Macdonell (ed.). Delhi: Motilal Banarsidass.

Bṛhaspati-sūtra. 1921. F.W. Thomas (ed.). Delhi: Motilal Banarsidass

Chhāndyogya Upaniṣad. 1956. Durgacharan Saṁkhya-Vedānta-tīrtha (ed. & tr.). Calcutta.

Daśakumāra-carita (of Daṇdin). 1875 (Śāka era). Haridāsa Siddhāntavāgīśa (ed.). Calcutta.

Gautamapraṇītadharmasūtrāṇī. 1949. Ānandāśrama Saṁskrita Series, No. 61.

Halāyudhakośa. 1958. Jayashamkara Joshi (ed.). Varanasi: Sarasvati Bhavan.

The Jātaka-māla (of Aryasura). J.S. Speyer (tr.). Delhi: Motilal Banarsidass.

Jātaka. 1385-87 (Śāka era). Isan Chandra Ghosh (tr.). Calcutta: Karuna Prakashani.

Kādambarī (of Bāṇabhatta). 1872 (Śāka era). Haridas Siddhāntavāgīśa (ed. & tr.). Calcutta.

Katyāyana-śrauta-sūtra. 1989 (Samvat era). Vidyādhara Sarma (ed.). Kāśī: Achyuta-Granthamala.

Khadiragṛhasūtra. (Bibliotheca Sanskrita No. 41). A. Mahadeva Sastri and L. Srinivasacharya (eds.). Mysore.

The Mahābhārata. Poona: Bhandarkar Oriental Research Institute.

Maitryanī-Saṁhitā. 1883. 4 Vols. Leophold Von Schroeder (ed.). Leipzig.

Manusmṛti. 1939. 2 Vols. Ganganath Jha (ed.). The Asiatic Society of Bengal.

Mṛchhakatikam. 1878 (Śāka era). Haridas Siddhāntavāgīśa (ed. & tr.). Calcutta.

Nighanṭu. See *Niruktam*.

Niruktam. 1970. 4 Vols. Amareswar Thakur (ed. & tr.). University of Calcutta.

Pāṇini. See *Aṣṭādhyāyīsūtrapathaḥ*; also Kasikavāmana Jayāditya's Commentary. 1931. Pandit Ananta Sāstri Phādki (ed.).

Patañjali. See *Vyākaraṇa-mahābhāṣya*.

Srimad-Vālmīki-Rāmāyanam. 1958. 2nd edn. K. Chinnaswami Sastrigal (ed.). Madras.

Die Hymnen des Regveda. 1955. 2 Vols. 3rd edn. T. Aufrecht (ed.). Akedemie-Verlag. Berlin.

Ṛgveda Brāhmṇas: *The Aitareya and Kausītaki Brāhmaṇas of the Ṛgveda*. 1920. Harvard Oriental Series, No. 25, A.B. Keith (tr.).

Śabda-kalpa-druma. 1961. Delhi: Motilal Banarsidass.

The Hymns of the Samaveda. 1963. Ralph T.H. Griffith (tr.). Varanasi: Chowkhambha.

The Sāṅkhyāyana-Āraṇyaka (With an Appendix on the *Mahavrata*). 1908. A.B.V. Keith, London.

The Sarva-darśana-saṁgraha. 1961. E.B. Cowell, and A.E. Gough (eds.). Varanasi: Chowkhamba.

Śāśvatakośa or *The Anekārthasamuchchaya of Śāśvata*. Narayan Nathji Kulkarni (ed.). Pune: Oriental Book Agency.

Śatapatha Brāhmaṇa. Vol. 26, Pt. III. Sacred Books of the East.

Smṛtinām Samuchchaya. 1929. Anandasrama Sanskrit Series, No. 48. V.G. Apte (ed.).

Śrauta-kośa. 1958. Pune: Vaidika Samsodhana Mandala.

Srivasisthadharma Śāstram. 1930. Alois Anton Fuehrer (ed.). Pune: B.O.R.I. Institute.

The Taittiriya Brāhmaṇa. 1911. Bibliotheca. Sanscritica No. 38. A, Mahadeva Sastri and I. Srinivasacharya (eds.). Mysore.

Vaikhanasasmārta Sūtram. 1927. W. Caland (ed.). Calcutta: The Asiatic Society of Bengal.

The Vajrasūcī of Aśvaghoṣa: *A Study of the Sanskrit Text and Chinese Version*. 1960. 2nd edn. Sujit Kumar Mukhopadhyaya (tr.). Santiniketan.

Vāsiṣṭhasmṛti. See *Smṛtinām Samuchchaya*.

Vyākaraṇa-mahābhāṣya (of Patañjali). 1967. Delhi: Motilal Banarsidass.

Yajurveda Saṁhitā. Damodara Satvalekar (ed.). Bombay.

Yamasmṛti. See *Smṛtinām Samuchchaya*.

Yāska. See *Niruktam*.

B. Secondary Literature

The Age of Imperial Unity. 1960. Vol. II. Bambay: Bharatiya Vidya Bhavan.

Ambedkar, B.R. 1969. *The Untouchables*. Shravasti, Balarampur: Jetavan Mahavihar.

Beal, Samuel. 1869. *Travels of Fa-Hien and Sung-Yun*. London: Trubner and Co.

Bhandarkar, D.R. 1940. *Some Aspects of Ancient Indian Culture* (Sir William Meyer Lectures, 1938-39). University of Madras.

———. 1969. *Aśoka*. University of Calcutta.

Bose, Atindranath. 1942. 2 Vols. *Social and Rural Economy of Northern India*. University of Calcutta.

Bühler, G. 1886. *The Laws of Manu*. Oxford: Clarendon Press.

Briggs, Geo. W. 1920. *The Chamers*. Calcutta: Association Press.

Burrow, T. 1955. *The Sanskrit Language*. London: Faber and Faber.

The Cambridge History of India. 1962. Vol. 1. Delhi: S. Chand & Co.

Chanana, Dev Raj. 1960. *Slavery in Ancient India*. New Delhi: People's Publishing House.

Chatterji, Suniti Kumar, 1974. *Kirata-Jana-Kirti: The Indo-Mongoloids: Their Contitutions to the History and Culture of India.*

Dattaray, R. 1974. *A Forgotten Functionary of Ancient India That Was Kṣattrī.* Calcutta: Sanskrit Pustak Bhandar.

Dutt, Nalinaksha. 1971. *Early Monastic Buddhism.* Calcutta: Firma K.L. Mukhopadhyaya.

Dutt, Nripendra Kumar. 1925. *The Aryanisation of India.* Calcutta.

———. 1931. *Origin and Growth of Caste in India.* Vol. 1. London: Kegan Paul, Trench, Trubner and Co., Ltd.

Fick, Richard. 1920. *The Social Organisation in North-east India in Buddha's Time.* Sishirkumar Mitra (trns.). University of Calcutta.

Fuchs, Stephen. 1950. *Children of the Hari: A Study of the Nimar Balahis of Madhya Pradesh.* Vienna: Verlag Herold.

Fuehrer-Haimendorf, Christoph von. See *Children of Hari* by Stephen Fuchs.

Gandhi, M.K. 1339 (Śāka era). *Hindu Dharma O Asprṛśyatā.* Bengali tr. by Satish Chandra Dasgupta. Sodepur.

———. 1927. *Young India.* 17 November.

Ghoshal, U.N. (n.d.). *A History of Hindu Public Life.* Pt. 1. Calcutta.

Ghurye, G.S. 1963. *The Scheduled Tribes.* Bombay: Popular Prakashan.

Gopal, Ram. 1959. *India of Vedic Kalpasutra.* Delhi: National Publishing House.

Goswami, K.G. 1936. *Prāgaitihāsik Mohenjodaro.* University of Calcutta.

Griswold, H.D. 1971. *The Religion of the Ṛgveda,* Delhi: Motilal Banarsidass.

Kane, P.V. 1930, 1941. *History of Dharmaśāstra.* Vols. I & II. Pt. 1. Poona: Bhandarkar Oriental Research Institute.

Kosambi, D.D. 1952. "Ancient Kosala and Magadha" in the *Journal of the Bombay Branch of the Royal Asiastic Society.* Vol. XXVII, Pt. 2.

———. 1955. "The Working Class in the Amarakośa" in the *Journal of Oriental Research.* Vol. XXIV, Pts. I-IV. Madras.

———. 1956. *An Introduction to the Study of Indian History.* Bombay: Popular Book Depot.

Lassen, Christian. 1847. *Indische Altertumskuude.* erster Band. Bonn.

Lynch, Owen M. 1974. *The Politics of Untouchability*. Delhi: National.

———. 1978. "Remembering the Remembered Village" in *Contribution to Indian Sociology*. Vol. 12. University of Delhi.

Macdonell, Arthur. 1962. *A History of Sanskrit Literature*. Delhi: Motilal Banarsidass.

———. 1963. *The Vedic Mythology*. Varanasi: Indological Book House.

Macdonell and Keith. 1958. *Vedic Index of Names and Subjects*. 2 Vols. Delhi: Motilal Banarsidass.

Majumdar, R.C. 1960. *The Classical Acccounts of India*. Calcutta: Firma K.L. Mukhopadhyaya.

Mathai, M.O. 1978. *Reminiscences of the Nehru Age*. New Delhi: Vikas Publishing House.

Mayrhoffer, Manfred. 1958. *A Concise Etymological Sanskrit Dictionary*. Heidelberg: Band I, Carl Winter-Universitacts Verlag.

Mitra, Veda. 1956. *India of Dharmasūtras*. Delhi: Arya Book Depot.

McCrindle, J.W. 1973. *Ancient India as Described by Ktesias the Knidiau*. Delhi: Manohar.

Monier-Williams, Sir Monier. 1951. *A Sanskrit-English Dictionary*, Clarendon Press, Oxford (First edition 1899).

Mukherjee, Prabhati. 1974. "Toward Identification of Untouchable Groups in Ancient India as Enumerated in Sanskrit Lexicons" in the *Journal of the Asiatic Society*. Vol. XVI. Calcutta.

———. 1978. *Hindu Women: Normative Models*. New Delhi: Orient Longman.

———. 1981. "Some Notes on Panca: An Historical Enigma" in the *Journal of the Indian Anthropological Society*. Vol. 16, No. 1. Calcutta.

———. 1982. Review article on R.S. Sharma's *Sudras in Ancient India* in the *Journal of the Indian Anthropological Society*. Vol. 17. No. 2. Calcutta.

———. 1986. "Status Determinants in Early Brahmanical Literature: A Note" in *Determinants of Social Status in India*. (ed.) S.C. Malik. Shimla: Indian Institute of Advanced Study.

———. 1985. "A Passage to India", in the *Journal of the Economic and Social History of the Orient*. Vol. XXIX. Leiden.

Mukherjee, Ramkrishna. 1957. *The Dynamics of a Rural Society: A Study of the Economic Structure in Bengal Villages*. Berlin: Akademie-Verlag.

Oppert, Gustav. 1972. *The Original Inhabitants of India*. Delhi: Oriental Publishers.

Piggott, S. 1950. *Prehistoric India*. London: Pelican Books.

Rhys Davids. 1932. *A Manual of Buddhism*. London: The Sheldon Press.

Ruben, Walter. 1954. *Einfuerung in die Indienkunde*. Berlin: Deutscher Verlag der Wissenschaften.

———. 1957. *Die Lage der Sklaven in der Altindischen Gesellschaft*. Berlin: Akademie-Verlag.

———. "India's Fight Against Vṛtra in the Mahābhārata" in *S.K. Belvalkar Felicitation Volume*.

Sangave, Vilas Adinath. 1959. *Jaina Community: A Social Survey*. Bombay: Popular Book Depot.

Sharma, R.S. 1980. Śūdras in Ancient India. Delhi: Motilal Banarsidass.

Sitaramayya, B. Pattabhi. 1946. *The History of the Indian National Congress*. Vol. 1. Bombay: Padma Publications.

Stutley, Margaret and James. 1977. *A Dictionary of Hinduism: Its Mythology, Folklore and Development, 1500 B.C.-A.D.* 1500. Bombay: Allied Publishers.

Thapar, Romila. 1963. *Aśoka and the Decline of the Mauryas*. Delhi: Oxford University Press.

———. 1966. *A History of India*. Vol. II. London: Pelican Books.

———. 1979. *The Past and Prejudice*. National Book Trust (India).

Vasu, S.C. 1962. *The Aṣṭādhyayī of Paṇini*. 2 Vols. Delhi: Motilal Banarsidass.

Vigasin, A.A. and A.M. Somozvantsev. 1985. *Society, State and Law in Anciet India*. New Delhi: Sterling Publishers.

Zachariae, Theodor. 1897. *Die Indischen Worterbuecher* (Kosa). Strassburg: Verlag Von J. Trubner.

INDEX

Abhidhānaratnamālā, 57; *see also Halāyudhakośa*
ābhīra, 32, 39
Ācārangasūtra, 85
Age of Imperial Unity, 72
Agni, 99
Agnipurāna, 40
Agriculture, 32
Ait. Br., 29, 33
ajapāla, 32
Ājivakas, 2
Akṣamālā, 86
Amarakośa, 46, 49, 54, 57, 58, 59, 60, 90, 106
Ambaṣṭha, 44, 45, 46, 50
Ambedkar, B.R., 4, 5, 6, 7, 11, 12, 75, 91, 98, 105
amedhys, 40
āndhra, 33, 39
Anekārtha-samuchhaya see Śāśvatakośa
Āṅgiras, 58, 107
Āṅgirasa, 61, 90
Āṅgirasasmṛti, 61, 107
antajāti, 58, 59, 60
antapāla, 70
antavāsayin, 6, 57, 58, 59, 61, 62, 70, 90, 107
antevāsin, 57, 58, 107
antyaja, 58, 59, 60, 61, 107
antyavāsayin, 49, 70, 90
Anu, 26
anuloma, 43, 51, 52, 53, 55, 88, 89, 106
apapātra, 41
Āpastambiya-dharma-sūtra, 40, 41, 107; *Common*, 42
araṇyacāra, 38, 41, 68, 73, 100
Arthaśāstra, 14, 38, 39, 40, 41, 42, 45, 48, 50, 51, 52, 54, 55, 56, 63, 68, 70, 71, 72, 73, 74, 75, 84, 89, 90, 91, 92, 93, 94, 95, 98, 99, 105, 107
Arya(s), 14, 17, 18, 19, 20, 21, 22, 23, 24, 26, 27, 28, 30, 31, 32, 33, 34, 35, 38, 41, 71, 76, 78, 79, 80, 82, 85, 86, 90, 99, 103, 106; social organization of, 81, 83
aryaṇivāsa, 71
Aśoka, 3, 7, 38, 100, 102
Aṣṭādhayāyī, 31, 32, 37, 84
Aṣṭavimsttitattvam, 107
aśuci, 40
Asura(s), 20, 24, 26, 27, 31, 33, 76, 79, 80, 81, 82, 85, 102
aśvapa, 32
Āśvalāyanagṛhyasūtra, 30
aṭavika(s), 3, 38, 64, 70, 75, 86, 99, 100, 101, 103, 104
Atharvaveda, 25, 27, 29, 33, 106
Atri, 61
Atriṁhitā, 61
Aupamanyava, 26, 35, 106
ayagava, 59, 89, 91
ayogu, 24, 33, 55
āyogava, 47, 48, 54, 55, 56, 60, 62, 91

Bailey, 12
Bāṇabhatta, 63
bard/reciter, 22
bārudha, 32, 58, 59
Baudhāyana-dharma-sūtra, 30, 33, 41, 42, 44, 47, 50, 107
Baudhāyana-gṛhya-sūtra, 29, 40
Beal, Samuel, 41, 71
Bekanatan, 20, 21
Bhāgavata, 87
Bhakti movement, 2, 3
Bhandarkar, D.R., 38, 71, 100, 101, 106
bhāta, 58
Bhilla, 12, 58, 59
bhiṣak, 22
Bhujjya kṣataka, 44

bidalakāra, 24, 25
Bonnerjee, W.C., 10
Bose, Atindranath, 12, 92, 101, 102,
bhīṣak, 22
Brāhmaṇa(s), 3, 6, 7, 9, 13, 24, 29, 31, 35, 40, 41, 42, 51, 52, 63, 65, 66, 67, 68, 69, 70, 72, 73, 74, 75, 76, 81, 83, 88, 89, 90, 91, 95, 96
Brāhmanism, 6, 87
Bṛhad-āraṇyaka-Upaniṣad, 33, 53
Bṛhaddevatā, 25, 32, 86
Bṛhadratha, 19
Bṛhaspati, 2
Bṛhaspati-sūtra, 71
Briggs Geo. W., 3, 12
Buddha, 2, 3, 21
Buddhism, 6, 7, 84, 87
Burrow, T., 80

Cambridge History of India, 88
caṇḍāla(s), 2, 12, 24, 32, 33, 36, 38, 39, 40, 41, 42, 47, 48, 49, 50, 53, 55, 56, 57, 58, 59, 60, 62, 63, 64, 65, 67, 68, 69, 70, 71, 72, 74, 75, 76, 77, 83, 86, 87, 88, 89, 90, 91, 92, 93, 94, 98, 99, 100, 101, 102, 103, 104, 107; *-ballaki*, 102; *-bhāsā*, 102; *-kānda*, 102; *vaṁśadhopana*, 102
carmakāra, 58, 59, 60, 101
carman, 32, 33
Cārvāka, 2
caste, 3, 5, 6, 7, 9, 14
Chanana, Dev Raj, 70
Chatterjee, Suniti Kumar, 106
Chhāndyogya-Upaniṣad, 33, 106
Christian(s), 9, 10
Cohn, 12
Cucaka, 44

Dāsa(s), 17, 18, 19, 20, 24, 25, 27, 28, 33, 34, 59, 71, 79, 82, 83, 98, 101, 106
Daśa-kumāra-carita, 60, 67, 69
Dasyu(s), 18, 20, 24, 25, 74, 79, 82, 101, 106
Dattaray, R., 54, 89
Dausyānta, 44
depressed class, 10, 11
Deva, 26, 27
dhanuskāra, 24, 25
Dhavira, 47
dhīvara, 24, 32, 59
divākirti, 30, 57, 58
domba(s), 32, 37, 39, 41, 83, 86, 91, 92, 98
Droṇa, 42, 77
Druhyu, 26
Dutt, Nalinaksh, 2
Dutt, Nripendra Kumar, 29, 33, 40, 42, 53
dvija, 24, 41, 51, 55, 83, 90, 101

Elliot, Sir H.M., 105

Fa-Hien, 41, 93, 94
Fick, Richard, 12, 72, 75, 88, 98, 100, 102
Freedman, 12
Fuchs, Stephen, 12
Furer Haimendorf, Christopher Von, 13

Galanter, 14
Gāndharva, 26
Gandhi, M.K., 4, 5, 7, 8, 9, 10, 11, 12, 105
Gautama-dharma-sūtra, 40, 44, 47, 94
ghettos, 67
ghoṣa, 71
Ghoshal, U.N., 29
Ghurye, G.S., 4, 10
Gonds, 92
gopa, 95
Gopal, Ram, 29
gopāla, 22, 24
Goswami, K.G., 23
grama, 71, 72, 73, 74
grāmika, 95, 97
gṛhapa, 32
Griswold, H.D., 26
grua, 56
Gupta, 10, 11, 105

Halāyudhakośa, 57, 58, 59, 60, 61, *see also Abhidhānaratnamālā*
Haradatta, 107
Harijan, 8, 105
hastips, 32
Herdotus, 108
hina-kula, 22
Hinduism, 8, 10
hiraṇya, 106
hiraṇyakāra (goldsmith), 24, 25
Hutton, 92

Indian National Congress, 4, 9, 10, 11
Indra (Lord), 19, 20, 21, 79
inter-*varṇa* marriages, 43, 56; table of, 44-50
Iranian Dāha and Dahyu, 106
iṣukāra, 24, 25

Jainism, 84, 87
jananggama, 57, 58, 59
janapada, 75
Jātakas, 63, 67, 71, 72, 73, 74, 75, 76, 91, 92, 93, 94, 95, 99, 100, 102
Jātakamālā, 73
jāti, 8, 96, 105
Journal of the Asiatic Society, 107

Kabīr, 3
Kādambarī, 41, 63, 67, 68, 69, 70, 71, 77
Kaivarta, 32, 56, 58, 59, 72, 73, 88
Kandaloi, 12, 91, 94
Kane, P.V., 41, 71, 91, 92, 107
kāpālika, 92
Karaṇa, 44, 45, 52
karma, doctrine of, 96
karmakāra, 72, 73
karmāra, 22, 24
Karṇa, 100
Kaśika-Vāmana-Jayāditya, 107
Kaṭh, 87
Kātyāna-śrauta-sūtra, 29, 30, 40, 53
Kauśika, 65, 66, 67, 77
Kauṭilya, 14, 38, 40, 42, 45, 48, 50, 51, 52, 68, 70, 74, 84, 94, 96, 98, 100, 105, 107
Keith, 19, 20, 21, 22, 33, 42, 80, 81, 101
Khadira-gṛhya-sūtra, 30
Kīkaṭa, 21, 22, 34
kirāta(s), 24, 25, 33, 34, 38, 39, 57, 58, 59, 64, 67, 68, 69, 70, 76, 85, 90, 100, 101, 103
kitaba, 24
Kosambi, D.D., 14, 20, 23, 24, 26, 57, 73, 81, 88, 97, 100, 106
kṣatra, 32, 33, 47, 54
Kṣatriya(s), 9, 42, 51, 53, 72, 74, 75, 87, 89, 90, 96, *see also* Rājanya
kṣatta, 47, 48, 49, 53, 54, 55, 59, 62, 89, 90, 91
kṣattar(s), 83
kṣattrī, 47, 48, 50
kṣuramarḍin, 58
ksurin, 30, 57
kutāla, 32

Lassen, Christian, 26, 55, 91, 92, 102, 106
Latyāyana-śrauta-sūtra, 29
lubdhaka, 38, 64
Lynch, Owen M., 12, 14, 98, 105

Macdonell, Arthur A., 19, 20, 21, 22, 33, 37, 42, 57, 58, 80, 81, 101, 106
Madgu, 44
madiga, 92
māgadha, 24, 47, 48, 49, 54, 55, 56, 59, 62, 88, 89, 90, 91
Magadhan(s), 79, 80, 81, 83, 88
Mahābhārata, 42, 45, 52, 60, 64, 65, 67, 68, 69, 71, 76, 86, 92
Mahanarma, 44
māhiṣya, 44, 45, 52
Majumdar, R.C., 39
māla, 58
maṇikāra (jeweller), 24, 25
Manu, 27, 43, 51, 52, 53, 54, 63, 69, 70, 86, 88, 102; lawbook of, 7
Manusmṛti, 7, 31, 40, 41, 45, 48, 50, 51, 52, 53, 54, 56, 63, 64, 68, 69, 70, 71, 91, 92, 93, 94, 97, 98, 107
margara, 33

Mātaṅga, 67, 69, 77
mātaṅga(s), 41, 57, 58, 60, 64, 67, 69, 70, 71, 77, 87, 92, 101
mātaṅgarāja, 87
mātaṅga-jāti-sparśa-doṣa, 41
Mayrhoffer, Manfred, 102
McCrindle, J.W., 39, 68, 69, 70, 76
meda, 58, 59
Medhātithi, 27, 63, 93
Memoirs of the Races of the North Western Provinces of India, 105
Mencher, 12
mixed-*varṇa*, 27, 33, 42, 43, 53, 56, 62, 65, 88, 89, 90, 101; *see also varṇa-saṁkara*
mlechha(s), 38, 39, 57, 58, 59, 70, 76, 85, 90, 102
Moffat, 12
Mrchhakatikam, 71
Mṛgayu (deer-hunter), 24, 25
mṛtapa(s), 32, 37, 39, 41, 71, 83, 86, 91, 92, 98
Muir, 106
Mukherjee, Prabhati, 96, 105, 106
Muṇḍās, armed uprisings of, 4
Muṇḍin, 30, 57
Mūrdhavasikta, 44, 45
Muslims, 9, 10
mutiba, 33

nagara, 71, 72, 73, 97
nahala, 58
Namuci, 19
napita(s), 28, 30, 50, 57, 58, 76, 82, 83, 89, 90
Nārada, 87
Nārada Smṛti, 7
nata, 58, 59
Navavastu, 19
neo-Buddhism, 5
nīca-śākhā, 22, 80
nīca-vaṁśa, 22
nigama, 72, 73
Nighaṇṭu, 21, 106
Nirukta, 14, 20, 21, 22, 26, 27, 29, 31, 32, 33, 64, 76, 78, 84
niṣāda(s), 24, 26, 27, 28, 29, 30, 32, 35, 39, 41, 42, 44, 45, 46, 51, 52, 56, 57, 58, 61, 64, 65, 72, 73, 76, 77, 82, 83, 85, 88, 89, 90, 99, 101
nistya, 58
non-violence, 66
Nṛpa, 44

Oppert, Gustav, 12, 76, 92, 102

palli, 72
pañca, 26, 27, 34, 35, 82
pañcajana, 26, 27, 28
pañcajāti, 26
pañcakati, 26
pañca kṛṣti, 26
pañcama, 101, 102, 106
pañcamānava, 27
Pāṇini, 14, 31, 32, 37, 39, 41, 72, 84
Paṇi(s), 19, 20, 24, 32, 34, 38, 76, 79, 80, 81, 82
pāraśava/Naiṣāda, 44, 45, 52, 89
pāṣanda, 92
Patañjali, 14, 32, 71, 84, 85, 91
paulkasa/pulkasa, 24, 32, 33, 36, 47, 49
Piggott, S., 23, 24, 38
Pipru, 20
Pitṛ, 26
plava, 57, 58, 59
plough-maker, 22
Pracinasala, 106
pradeṣṭṛ, 95
Pramaganda, 21, 22
pratiloma, 13, 27, 43, 53, 54, 55, 56, 57, 59, 61, 62, 68, 89, 90, 91, 100, 106, 107
pratyanta grāma, 72
pratyanta pradeśa, 72, 74
Protective Discrimination, policy of, 4
Ptolemy, 12, 91, 94, 102, 106
pukkasa, 57, 58, 60
pulinda(s), 12, 33, 38, 39, 57, 58, 59, 64, 67, 68, 70, 77, 85, 90, 100, 103
pṇḍra, 33, 39
punjistha (fowler), 24, 25
purity-pollution theory, 7, 13, 98, 99, 105
Pūru, 26

Raghunandan, 107
Rāi Dās, 3
rajaka, 58, 59, 60, 101, *pallies* of, 72
Rājanya, 24, 81; *see also* Kṣatriya(s)
Rajavahana, 77
Rākṣasa(s), 19, 20, 24, 26, 27, 31, 34, 79, 80, 81, 82, 106
Rāma, 77, 85
Ramaka, 49
Rāmāyana, 29, 68, 85
Rantideva, 66
rathakāra(s), 22, 24, 28, 29, 30, 41, 42, 44, 50, 51, 52-53, 56, 76, 82, 83, 89, 90
revenue, sources of, 95
Ṛgveda, 14, 17, 18, 19, 20, 21, 22, 23, 24, 25, 26, 27, 28, 29, 30, 31, 32, 33, 36, 38, 62, 75, 101, 106, 107
Rhys, Davids, 2
Risley, 105
Ruben, Walter, 12, 19, 24, 37, 70, 108

sabadāhaka(s), 91, 92, 98
śabara(s), 33, 38, 39, 57, 58, 59, 64, 67, 69, 70, 85, 86, 90, 99, 100, 101, 103
Śabdakalpadruma, 40, 41, 55, 58, 59, 60, 61, 62, 64, 69
śailusa (dancer), 24
samāhatṛ, 95
Sāmaveda, 24, 26
Sambara, 18
Sāṁkhyāyana Āranyaka, 33
samvaha, 71
saṇḍāla, 92
Sangave, Vilas Adinath, 102, 106
Sāntāls, 4, 104
Sāntāl Rebellion (1855), 4
sārameya, 38
Sarva-darśana-saṁgraha, 2
Sarvārthaciṇtaka, 97
Sastri, Ganapati, 39
Śāśvatakośa, 45, 48, 57, 59, 60
Śatapatha Brāhmana, 76
Satyakāma, 87
Savarṇa, 44, 45
Scheduled Castes and Tribes, 1, 3, 4, 11
Scheduled Districts Act (1874), 4
Sharma, R.S., 6, 12, 21, 56, 63, 94, 98, 102, 105, 106
Sikhs, 10
Sitaramayya, B. Pattabhi, 5, 8, 10, 11
Skandaswami, 27
Slaves, 2, 12, 13, 28
Smṛitināmsamuccaya, 107
śrāddha, performance of, 96
Śrauta kośa, 40
śreṣṭhis, 63, 72, 74, 93
Statesman, 1
sthanika, 95
Stutley, Margaret, 39, 107, 108
Śūdra(s), 2, 9, 24, 25, 31, 34, 35, 37, 40, 41, 42, 45, 51, 52, 55, 65, 72, 74, 75, 81, 82, 83, 85, 86, 89, 90, 91, 94, 97, 101, 102, 106
śuna-mukha, 39, 70
surākāra, 32
Suṣṇa, 20
suta(s), 24, 32, 33, 47, 48, 49, 53, 54, 55, 56, 59, 62, 83, 89, 90, 91, 103
sūtradhāra, 72, 73
Śvaganika, 38
svaganin(s), 38, 64, 68, 70, 85
śvan/śvanita, 24, 38
śvapaca(s), 32, 38, 39, 40, 41, 53, 55, 57, 58, 59, 60, 61, 62, 63, 64, 68, 69, 70, 76, 83, 86, 88, 89, 91, 100, 103
śvapāka, 48
śvapati, 38
sydroi, 106

Taittirīya Brāhmana, 24, 33, 36
takṣman (wood-curver), 22, 24, 25, 32
tantuvaya, pallies of, 72
Thapar, Romila, 38, 80, 81
Tribes and Castes of Bengal, 105
Triśanku, 68, 69, 71
Turvasu, 18, 26, 27, 28
tvasta, 22, 24, 25, 79

ugra, 32, 33, 41, 44, 45, 50, 51, 52, 53, 83
untouchability, 1, 2, 3, 4, 5, 6, 7, 8, 10, 11, 12, 13, 14, 15, 63, 93, 98, 105
untouchables, 1, 2, 3, 4, 5, 6, 7, 8, 9, 10, 11, 12, 13, 14, 15, 16, 35, 40, 57, 59, 62, 63, 64, 67, 75, 86, 87, 91, 93, 94, 99, 105
Upamanyu, 106
Urvaśī, 86

Vaci or Vati, 19
vaideha, 48
vaidehaka(*s*), 47, 48, 49, 50, 52, 54, 55, 56, 59, 62, 88, 90, 91
Vaikhānasa samārta-sūtra, 44, 47, 50, 63, 69, 70, 71
vaiṇa/vaiṇys, 49, 53
Vaiśya(s), 5, 9, 24, 25, 31, 41, 42, 51, 52, 53, 55, 72, 74, 75, 81, 82, 83, 89, 90, 98, 106
Vajrasūci, 87
Valdahaka, 47
Vāmadeva, 107
van/araṇya/atavī, 72, 73
vanacara, 73, 100
vaṇijah, 32
vapta, 22, 30
varṇa dharma, 8, 9
varṇa system, 1, 2, 8, 96
varṇa-saṁkara, 13, 33, 42; *see also* mixed *varṇa*
Vasiṣṭha, 41, 86
Vāsiṣṭha smṛti, 30, 46, 49
Vasu, S.C., 37
veṇa, 52
Vidura, 76, 86
Vigasin, 94
Vipra, 31
Viṣṇu, 41
Viṣṇusmṛti, 94
Viśvāmitra, 33, 68, 71, 77, 87; story of, 60
Viśvarūpa, 107
Vratyas, 32
Vṛtra, 19
Vyākaraṇa-mahā-bhāṣya, 32, 71, 84, 91
Vyāsa, 86

Yadu, 18, 26, 27, 28
Yajurvedasaṁhitā, 24, 27, 29
Yama, 58, 61
Yamasmṛti, 61
Yāska, 21, 26, 31, 84, 85
Yavana, 44

Zachariase Theo-dor, 57, 58